For Jason, Liesl, and Welly,

the loves of my life

and the best running partners I could ever ask for

CONTENTS

PREFACE

A BUZZING THRONG of 50,869 runners stood on the blustery shores of Staten Island in their assigned corrals at the start line of the 44th running of the New York City Marathon on November 2nd, 2014. Hailing from 130 countries and all 50 states, it was the largest marathon in history. Ten thousand volunteers and two million eager spectators packed the streets and the subways of the Big Apple.

An already hectic morning was made more challenging by a vicious blast of Arctic air that dropped snow on Chicago and Detroit a couple days earlier and swept eastward, arriving in New England just in time for the race. Along with it came bone-chilling 40°F (4°C) winds that gusted upwards of 45 miles per hour.

Race organizers dismantled signage and tents in the start village to ground potential projectiles, while volunteers huddled together out of the wind. Race bibs and running caps were ripped right off the athletes and blasted skyward by the unrelenting gusts. All manner of race-day debris floated up into the ether.

Worried a wheeler might be overtaken by the wind, officials decided to move the start line of the wheelchair and handcycle races to the Brooklyn side of the Verrazano-Narrows Bridge, shortening the course to 23.2 miles. The double-decked suspension bridge that connects Staten Island and Brooklyn, which makes up much of the first 2 miles of the race, is particularly vulnerable to high winds due to its size and proximity to the open ocean. All the while, television crews throughout the city struggled to keep video feeds broadcasting to the world as their equipment was repeatedly toppled by the elements.

The type of searing wind that cuts through every layer of clothing, rattling your bones, freezing your blood, stinging your face, and drying your eyeballs, it was a categorically brutal morning for runners, spectators, media, organizers, and volunteers alike.

New York City Mayor Bill de Blasio was there to bolster the mood, wishing runners well at the start line: "To all the runners who fought hard to get to this day, like all New Yorkers, you're not going to let some cold or wind hold you back."

The nervous athletes bounced up and down in a fruitless attempt to warm up as the start time approached. They wore wool hats, old sweatshirts, and plastic bags, all to be shed once the race got going.

When the gun fired, the frontrunners took off over the bridge and soon settled into a rhythm well off record pace on account of the conditions. Stuck in the congestion, those in the middle and back of the pack moved at a snail's pace as they urged the tens of thousands of runners before them to push ahead.

On the bridges, crosswinds nearly picked runners up off their feet and blew them sideways. On the city streets, headwinds funneled between buildings, making striding forward at any speed an arduous task. As they made their way from Staten Island through Brooklyn, Queens, the Bronx, and to the finish line in Manhattan's Central Park, many struggled mightily against the frigid, face-slapping gales.

Meanwhile, Mary Wittenberg, race director and New York Road Runners (NYRR) CEO and president at the time, waited at the finish line for hours, trying to keep warm. Standing in that same spot many times since starting her tenure with NYRR in 1998, she'd seen a lot over the years. But at the 2014 finish line, she observed something particularly striking. The less-than-favorable conditions seemed to firmly place runners in two camps. In one, there were the athletes who appeared tense and miserable, grimacing as they crossed the line, and voicing their displeasure with the experience. In the other were the runners who looked relaxed, exhilarated, and unfazed by the weather, throwing their arms up with smiles plastered across their wind-burned faces.

"The contrast was so dramatic, I thought, 'how can there be two totally different experiences?'" Wittenberg recently told me from her office in New York City, where she now serves as CEO of Richard Branson's Virgin Sport. She offered this thought:

> *"I'm convinced that the runners who were more worried about their times and anxious about the conditions tensed up in that wind and fought it the whole way, while the others—runners of all paces, including many fast people—just focused on relaxing and enjoying a great run through New York. By staying relaxed, it was as if they weren't punished by the wind as much."*

As is true in many situations in both running and life, the harder you try to accomplish something through sheer force of will, the more difficult the task becomes. Instead of harboring keen awareness and intuition to gracefully navigate the constellation of interactions between body, brain, and environment in adverse conditions, we blindly rely on grit, toughness, and brute strength. While those skills aren't for naught, we end up employing them indiscriminately because we are so disconnected. The synchrony of mind, body, and spirit is lost.

I very much recognized myself in those overwrought runners from the story Wittenberg told me. I had once been the athlete who would get so focused on an end goal that I paid little attention to what was going on with my body and mind on the path to reaching that objective. Not only did that contribute to overtraining injuries, it also meant that when I ran, my unsupervised mind whirred at breakneck pace, needlessly cycling worries and other preoccupations. My gaze was always fixed on that clear objective on the horizon, but my day-to-day training sometimes felt more akin to motion blur in a photograph—hurried and frenetic—smeared around the margins of the image.

* * *

I grew up watching the Twin Cities Marathon in my hometown of Minneapolis, Minnesota every fall with my dad. We would get bundled up the first Sunday in October and stop at the gas station near our house to load up on hot chocolate and glazed donuts before heading to our favorite spot to cheer along the Minnehaha Creek, which flows through the south side of the city and eventually empties into the Mississippi River. Our annual outpost was near a house where the residents set up oversized speakers in their yard and blared upbeat music for the athletes. We would sit talking, eating, and offering high-fives to the runners. As a kid, I couldn't wait to someday run the race myself. I caught the running bug in a serious way along that roadside.

In the beginning, I ran simply because it was something I loved to do. The fresh air and freedom of movement drew me to the sport, but it was that feeling of pushing myself a little out of my comfort zone that kept me coming back. Running dialed me into life in a way nothing else did. For these same reasons, I ended up becoming a journalist and covering endurance sports as my main beat. I didn't just want to log miles myself, I also sought to learn what made other runners tick and share with readers their passion for this simple act of movement.

Years later, I was in graduate school working on my degree in sports and exercise psychology, immersed in studying how athletes get burned out when an activity becomes devoid of meaning and detached from intrinsic purpose. I learned that joy wanes and performance suffers when we get so hung up on our ultimate goals that we are no longer in wholehearted pursuit of process. I considered that I might serve as a good case study.

Wholly caught up in certain achievements—defending my master's thesis and training for the Boston Marathon topped my list at the time—I hardly took notice of my soaring stress levels. I was pushing, driving, and striving, with little time to rest en route. Running was supposed to be something that diffused stress in my life—I wasn't competing against anyone but myself, after all—but somehow it was contributing to it.

I knew that I'd be a happier and healthier runner if I got back to basics. So began my mindful running practice, although I didn't call it that at first. By definition, mindfulness is about upholding present moment awareness of the body, mind, and surroundings in a nonjudgmental manner. Mindful running is meditative movement—a process that trains you to exist in the moment with greater awareness as you run. It teaches you to lean in to experiences with superior intention and offers you agency when adjustments are necessary.

I discovered some immediate benefits when I applied the principles of mindfulness to running. Simply noticing the thoughts and emotions careening into my consciousness led to a natural easing of body and brain. I also got better at responding to physical cues—knowing when my legs were overcooked from a workout or if I was worn down from a busy week. It meant that I was getting injured less and training smarter, not harder. I also began to appreciate the brilliant sunrise over the lake near my apartment as I ran each morning. Had that always been there?

Perhaps best of all, many of the calming and focusing effects of my mindful running practice spilled over into the rest of my life. I was able to concentrate on my work more adeptly and handle life's slings and arrows with increasing ease.

***

While I harbor a healthy bit of skepticism for anything new-agey—energy vortexes, fortune telling, cosmic crystals, and the

Mindfulness can help train your body and brain to function optimally on a run.

like—I have more recently added seated meditation to my training routine. My husband, Jason, and I both have busy jobs and with a young daughter at home, I was no longer able to log the volume of mindful miles I once could, so I sought another activity by which I could relieve stress and cultivate that mindful state.

My primary hurdle to this was getting over the uninformed stereotypes I held on to about conventional meditation. For some reason, I had trouble shaking images of the dumb opening scene from the movie *Ace Ventura: When Nature Calls,* where Jim Carrey's character meditates in a Himalayan ashram on the edge of the Tibetan plateau, surrounded by monkeys, a llama, a tiger, and a falcon. Clad in monastic robes and a yellow headdress resembling a huge mohawk (what I now know is part of a Buddhist sect's traditional garb), Ace Ventura talks about obtaining "omnipresent super-galactic oneness" and a "medallion of spiritual accomplishment." I don't think I've ever even watched the entire thing, but for some reason, that scene from the cringe-worthy 1995 comedy stuck in my head.

I put those images aside and started by downloading a couple different guided meditation apps and trying to spend a few minutes sitting every other day or so. I found that it felt more like an intellectual exercise than an esoteric spiritual enterprise, so I ended up sticking with it. On days I couldn't squeeze in a run, I could usually find ten minutes to sit, take a few deep breaths, and listen to a guided meditation.

I reaped so much value from my brief sessions of seated meditation that I decided to take a course in Mindfulness-Based Stress Reduction (MBSR), a training program developed by Jon Kabat-Zinn, the founding executive director of the Center for Mindfulness at the University of Massachusetts Medical School, just outside of Boston. The course has been praised by everyone from Anderson Cooper to Oprah, so I figured that was good enough reason for me to give it a shot. Even so, my enduring preconceived notions about meditation made me worry that I might have just signed myself up for eight weeks of sitting in lotus position with a bunch of zenned-out ascetics listening to pan-flute ballads.

As it turned out, the class involved no cheesy music, incense, or chanting. Our instructor, Terry Pearson, a mindfulness meditation expert who studied with Kabat-Zinn, was a pharmacist with several decades of clinical experience and a master's degree in business. She started meditating over 20 years ago when she was serving in the Peace Corps in Zimbabwe and worked on a number of clinical research projects funded by the National Institutes of Health to measure the impact of MBSR. As it happens, I discovered she was also an avid runner who applied mindfulness to her training. The class of twelve comprised a couple school teachers, a college professor, a football coach, a lawyer, a university administrator, and a corporate buyer, among others.

The first day, Pearson presented us with a snow globe and tipped it upside down. The flakes floated around every which way, clouding our view of the Minnie Mouse character at the center of the scene. The snow, she said, represented the thoughts and emotions that often create a storm of chaos in our minds. I could definitely identify with that idea, particularly on the days I wasn't able to get out for a run.

"When the flakes settle at the bottom, that's when the mind is more peaceful and you can see things clearly, which allows for calmness and better decision-making," she said.

The ensuing eight-week course further enhanced my present-moment awareness and ability to concentrate. I have found that I don't get so easily pulled in to my own neurotic misadventures, ruminating about the past or obsessing about the future. Most runs I'm able to simply focus on my breathing and the rhythm of my stride and accept the fact that there will be moments of discomfort and suffering. This has made me a happier and healthier runner, but also a more switched-on human being in general.

Whether you're a complete novice or a veteran marathoner, the beauty of mindful running is that it allows you to notice when you're operating in autopilot and getting carried away by your thoughts and emotions. It can take you from being that runner with tense shoulders, a clenched jaw, and a clipped stride, fighting the wind every step of the way, to the one who, no matter what the weather, leans in to the gusts, puts one foot in front of the other, and performs at their best with joy and ease.

Mindful movement teaches you to engage in the moment and exist in the present.

INTRODUCTION

"Running is meditation for me. It puts me in a state of beautiful rhythm without any thought, will, push, or force. Every run is an opportunity to define myself. If you practice going into workouts and races with calm excitement and a sense of gratitude, not only will you have a healthier mindset, it also creates a chemical reaction in your body, which allows you to get the most out of a run or race."

THIS HAS ALWAYS been the type of thinking that pulls Deena Kastor out of just about any negative headspace during challenging moments of races. Consider mile 21 of the 2015 Chicago Marathon when she was suffering mightily. The dreaded wall that runners fear encountering loomed—that metaphorical barrier that makes you feel like you can't take another step. Sure enough, she ran right into it. Her energy levels plummeted, her hips tightened up and her hamstrings screamed. She could hear the bottoms of her shoes noisily slapping the pavement underfoot—she no longer felt like the light and swift three-time Olympian that she was.

Then a little voice inside her head launched a brutal assault: "You don't even want to be out here! What are you doing here?" Kastor recalled thinking when I spoke to her recently. "This hurts so badly! Your fastest days are well behind you. What are you out here trying to prove?"

To be sure, the 2004 Olympic bronze medalist and the American record holder in the marathon and half marathon couldn't expect to improve upon her 2 hour 19 minute 36 second personal best. Running at 5 minute 19 second mile pace for 26.2 miles was a thing of the past for the now 42-year-old mom, motivational speaker, and sports broadcaster. She also couldn't expect to compete for the win as she had exactly a decade earlier on the streets of the Windy City, where she snagged her first major marathon title. She couldn't even hope to likely place in the top five.

So, perhaps that voice wasn't so crazy after all. What the heck was she doing out there?

Then another voice interjected: "Wait a second. This is the part you like!" she thought to herself. "This is why you push the limits—to get to this point you're at right now—to find a stronger side to yourself. You need to find a way to get through this moment."

That thought jolted her out of that place of anxiety and self-reproach and back into the present. This wasn't the first time that she had doubts, yet she always kept moving forward.

"Even when a mile feels bad, I remind myself that it doesn't necessarily mean that is how the rest of the race is going to feel," she told me from her home in Mammoth Lakes, California. "There are good miles and bad miles, so in that moment, I told myself to just focus on that mile in front of me."

A long-time subscriber to the principles of mindfulness as they apply to running and life, this is a mindset she frequently returns to in the toughest moments of both. Rather than resisting discomfort as that initial voice urged her to do, she discovered that when she embraces the whole of the running experience and coexists with suffering, she is better able to find a way forward.

"Being mindful helps me in both the good and bad moments," she told me. "It's like when you feel fearful and as soon as you move past that fear, instead of being a fearful person, you're now a brave person. When we get through those difficult moments, we become stronger and more courageous on the other side."

To be sure, Kastor is not one to shy away from things that are hard. Through mindfulness, she has discovered that inviting in the spectrum of experiences has allowed her to grow as a runner. "Being mindful and paying attention to things like my form, my breath, and my purpose for each run makes the process of training so much more worthwhile and fulfilling, but also more productive," she told me.

She says that the key is to practice being mindful in the easier moments, so you can slip into that mindset in the tough times. "If you practice focusing on and giving attention to the things you do each day, it eventually becomes your habit and then it gets easier to be mindful in stressful situations—to take things in stride with some grace when life throws a hurdle in your way."

As she pulled herself out of the depths of misery in Chicago that day in 2015, Kastor thought to herself, "Five miles to go; I've hurt for 5 miles before. I can get this done." She forged ahead and finished in 2 hours 27 minutes 47 seconds, good enough for seventh place. Although not a personal best, it shattered the American masters' record in the marathon.

Widely recognized for her signature positivity of mind, she emphasized the connection between optimism and mindfulness. "It isn't about being naïve and ignoring the fact that it's raining outside," she told me. "But rather, to take time to understand specific emotions in the moment and interpret them in a way that benefits you and allows for personal growth."

Through a lens of mindfulness, Kastor views the highs and the lows of the running life in a unique way. In fact, it's one of the major reasons she continues to compete into her 40s: "I still enjoy the challenge of figuring out what to do in any given moment in a race, especially the harder ones, because that helps me grow intellectually and emotionally. It's probably why I haven't retired."

It was her untethered mind that momentarily peddled self-defeating and negative thoughts at mile 21 of the marathon. Kastor has learned that by mindfully tuning in to the panorama of her experience in the present moment, both the pleasant and the unpleasant, she's better able to navigate the ups and downs of racing and life.

* * *

A thought leader in the science of self-mastery and mindfulness, psychiatrist Judson Brewer is fond of saying: "You're already awesome. Just get out of your own way!" By this, he means that we all have great potential to live happy and productive lives, but many of us sabotage ourselves and underperform. The philosopher and "Father of American Psychology" William James gave a lecture at the University of Edinburgh in 1901 in which he said: "Most people live in a very restricted circle of their potential being. They make use of a very small portion of their possible consciousness, and of their soul's resources in general, much like a man who, out of his whole bodily organism, should get into a habit of using only his little finger."

Perhaps worst of all, we do this without even realizing it. In what writer Maria Popova calls our culture's "epidemic of hurrying and cult of productivity," we fail to listen to our bodies, overworking our systems until we are tired and burned out. Likewise, we leave our minds to their own devices to unnecessarily whip up stress and anxiety. We make mile 21 of the marathon harder than it needs to be, which causes us to fail to reach our true potential. If only we could tune in and notice that we are often our own worst enemies. Fortunately, we don't have to be.

Unlike training practices that must be scaled to a runner's experience and fitness, mindful running is something just about any runner can benefit from. Fast, slow, veteran or newbie, running on serene forest paths or gritty urban streets—we can all use a little brain training.

Insights gathered in research labs and on running trails around the globe suggest that simply shifting the way you relate to the present moment while you run—by tuning into the full experience—you can achieve greater health and happiness in training and life. In the same way that running strengthens our bodies, mindfulness serves to fortify our minds. While meditation is the most oft-cited method by which to cultivate mindfulness, I knew from my own training that it was also possible to meditate on the run. So began my deep dive into the practice of mindful running.

As a writer, I'm like a dog with a bone when I get interested in a particular subject. I read everything there is to read and love navigating the labyrinth of scientific research. Best of all, under the auspices of journalism, I often get the chance to sit down with remarkable human beings whose expertise far exceeds my own.

In the name of mindful running, I wanted to know: When runners talk about their training being "spiritual" or "meditative," is it because it's the one place they truly exist in the present? Does an athlete have to be "in the moment" to run well? Is there anything wrong with simply tuning out and letting your mind wander on a run? Can having greater awareness of the range of physical, mental, and emotional experiences enhance our satisfaction of the training process? Is mindfulness diametrically opposed to achievement? Are running enjoyment and optimal performance inextricably linked? How might we take that magical headspace we often access on the run into our everyday lives? Am I committing some sort of divine transgression when I practice running meditation instead of the more sedentary variety?

In my quest for answers, I conferred with Olympic and Paralympic runners, national champions, weekend warriors, and highly recognized coaches. I wasn't just looking for anecdotes to back up the practice of mindful running, though; I wanted empirical evidence. So I scoured the academic research, separated astronomy from astrology, and talked with scientists who are part of a new generation of researchers at the forefront of integrative medicine, psychology, contemplative neuroscience, and the science of self-mastery. Their fascinating work is illuminating the important connections between body, mind, and spirit and the ways that mindfulness can actually influence the very architecture of the brain and the quality of our experiences.

This book is designed to share what I've learned and provide a path toward greater ease, awareness, focus, and joy through mindful running. I hope to convince you that, although not a panacea or substitute for medical advice or treatment, mindfulness can be one of the sharpest arrows in your quiver both on and off the running trails.

***

While mindfulness is rooted in Buddhism, it made its sojourn from East to West in the 1970s, thanks in large part to Jon Kabat-Zinn. Separating the practice from its spiritual underpinnings, he created the Mindfulness-Based Stress Reduction (MBSR) course, thereby introducing a secular application of the practice to a whole new audience. Nevertheless, the quasi-spiritual connotations of conventional meditation and hints of self-help gimmickry send many folks running in the opposite direction. The idea of applying mindfulness to something you're already doing, in this case running, is frequently an easier pill to swallow.

I am far from the first to apply mindfulness to running. Stories abound chronicling the ultrarunning Buddhists of ancient Tibet who, according to legend, would spend three years meditating in a cave, chanting and doing breathing exercises, before embarking on a spiritual quest to run upward of 200 miles (320 km) straight. Famous French explorer and Buddhist Madame Alexandra David-Neel reported three separate encounters with the legendary "Lung-Gom-Pa runners" during her 14 years spent living in Tibet in the early 1900s. In her book *Magic and Mystery in Tibet*, she wrote eloquently about coming across a "strange traveler" a monk wearing a robe and toga, weightlessly gliding across the landscape of the wild grassy region of the northern plateau with a calm gaze set on the horizon.

There are also the modern "marathon monks" of Japan who run and walk sometimes more than a marathon a day for 1,000 consecutive days, followed by nine days deprived of food, water, and sleep. Through this ritual, they seek spiritual enlightenment as they study and pray at various temples along the way.

As I began to ask around, it turned out that a whole lot of runners in the Western world, with whom I shared far more in

In the pursuit of fitness and competition, it's easy to lose sight of the present moment.

common than any monastic, were also practicing mindfulness. Interestingly, almost without exception, the scientists and researchers in the field of contemplative neuroscience I spoke with were all runners themselves. Every single one said they applied the principles of mindfulness to their training. I knew I was on to something.

These conversations alleviated my concern that my personal brand of moving meditation might be deemed illegitimate by mindfulness purists. Pearson, my MBSR teacher, told me, "It's important to train both the body and the mind—running and meditation teach us perseverance and discipline. When you hit that wall in a marathon, you have to figure out a way around it in that moment. It's no different than any other obstacle in life."

Indeed, the sport engages the mind in a deep and enigmatic way. "Running offers athletes especially fertile grounds to learn the concepts of mindfulness," professional coach and co-author of *Peak Performance: Elevate Your Game, Avoid Burnout, and Thrive with the New Science of Success*, Steve Magness, told me. "I think it provides a lot of the same benefits that meditating in a more traditional way does. Going for a run, listening to your breathing and focusing on something is easier for a lot of people than sitting and trying to do it."

Applying mindfulness to your running creates a bridge between body and brain. This is especially important for new runners or those who are notorious for ignoring the body's signals and running through injuries. "It's about simply resting in and being with whatever is happening on the run, which allows us to learn from our body's wisdom. There's a lot that we can learn from paying attention," Brewer, who also happens to be a runner, told me.

Just as important, the practice can help you discover or rediscover greater satisfaction in running. Neuroscientist Leslie Sherlin, who has run more than 20 marathons and is the co-founder of a San Francisco-based purveyor of brain training research, told me: "The value of applying mindfulness to my running is all about learning to enjoy my training more. It's about finding joy in the process, which becomes much more meaningful and enriching. Mindfulness allows me to be in every moment to really experience my runs."

Leaning into your emotions, thoughts, physical sensations, and experiences—the good, the bad, and the ugly—can be quite powerful. Running mindfully doesn't mean that you won't feel pain, discomfort, or disappointment, but rather that you'll relate to those things in a different way. Instead of being completely derailed by adversity, mindfulness trains resilience and dynamism. What's more, in the most thrilling moments on the roads and trails—those times when everything clicks and your body works in perfect synchrony—mindfulness serves to imbue those runs with greater meaning.

***

The late George Sheehan was a cardiologist and author best known as the foremost philosopher of running. His 1978 book, *Running and Being: The Total Experience*, spent more than 14 weeks on the *New York Times* bestseller list and had a hand in inspiring the running boom of the 1970s and 1980s. In it, he wrote that he tackles each run with fresh eyes and a child-like wonder, "Hoping for a new appreciation of the landscape, a new perspective of my inner world, some new insights on life, a new response to existence and myself."

Tuning in to the moment has a way of giving you a fresh outlook on even the most well-worn trail. I hope this book can serve as a road map of sorts for happier, healthier, and more successful running by offering a new way to approach training. With any luck, the methods of mindfulness you learn through running will also positively influence the landscape of your life in a meaningful way.

Regardless of where you're at in your running practice, the mindful running process is the same: We *focus* in on the body, mind, and surroundings and become aware of thoughts, feelings, and sensations as they exist in the moment; we *fathom* that information by considering how it all fits together from a holistic standpoint and decide if we need to take any action; and when we follow these steps, we cultivate the conditions necessary to enter *flow*, a state that embodies present-moment awareness, concentration, confidence, and joy.

In Chapter 1, we'll look at the emerging scientific research espousing the benefits of aerobic exercise and mindfulness meditation. Thanks to improved brain-scanning techniques and other advances, there is evidence that the mindful state of being can influence everything from immune function, to inflammation, to

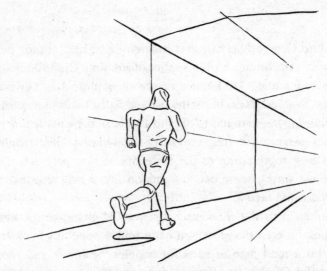

Running toward a more mindful state can enhance your training no matter where you run.

the very wiring of our brains. When integrated into aerobic training, which comes with a whole host of its own remunerations, the practice packs a powerful punch in terms of influencing well-being. If you are more concerned with the "how" of mindful running than the "why," go ahead and flip straight to Chapter 2 to get started.

In order to fully garner the benefits of mindful running, you must first make it a regular practice. In Chapter 2, we'll explore one of the toughest elements of any exercise program: motivation. I'll demonstrate how to be intentional about goal setting to get you started, but also keep you going over the long haul.

We will dive into the first step of mindful running in Chapter 3, which is *focus*. You will learn how to dial into present moment awareness as you run, becoming more attuned to your body, your mind, and the world around you.

Chapter 4 is all about helping you make calculated decisions about how, or whether, to respond to the things you observed in Step One. To *fathom* things as they are in the present, you will ascertain how to make more resolute choices. This step will also offer you a new perspective on how the machinations of body, mind, and environment interact and work together.

If you stop reading there, you'll already have the bulk of the knowledge you need to become a more mindful runner. But if you proceed to Step Three in Chapter 5, you'll learn how a mindful running practice can help you cultivate the sublime state of *flow*. We'll also look at the many ways mindfulness sets the scene for optimal performance.

For the more competitive harriers, Chapter 6 provides tips on how to apply your mindful running practice to racing. Contrary to popular belief, mindfulness is not antithetical to achievement. Whether you're an experienced marathoner or running your first 5K, the advice applies to every runner.

Chapter 7 chronicles the ways in which mindful running serves to teach you about life far beyond running. Comprised of sentiments from the runners and scientists I interviewed, they offer thoughts on the greater power of mindful running.

Finally, Chapter 8 includes a quick-start for mindful running—a cheat sheet of sorts for the practice. It also contains a mindful yoga routine, basic seated and walking meditations, and a few mindfulness hacks that can serve as anchors to the present moment in your daily life.

In 1977, David Shainberg, a renowned psychoanalyst, author and runner, published a paper in the *Annals of the New York Academy of Sciences*, where he wrote:

> *"Long distance running as meditation has a particular place in our world because it provides a special opportunity to understand the action of time, our relationship in space and movement … when I put on my track shoes, I feel like I am slipping into the comfortable realness of my body … And I cease to desire to have everything be easy at every moment and I accept that this is work and effort."*

He gets to the heart of mindful running, a practice that will teach you to welcome the whole of the running experience and relate to the things you observe in a fresh way. I like to say that mindful running can take you from zoom to zen. It is in the zen where ease, fluidity, focus, poise, and authenticity live. Time to lace up and get started.

Chapter 1
THE SCIENCE OF MINDFULNESS AND RUNNING

"I focused on each step and every breath even if they were a little worn. I arrived at the point in the race that I live for, the simple moments when you've reached down to your core and all you can do is keep running. I dreamt of this happening for months, waiting for the heart to take over."

THESE ARE THE words of Timothy Olson in his post-race account for the popular ultrarunning website, iRunFar after his record-setting first-place finish at the Western States Endurance Run in 2012. He shifted into this state around mile 80 when he left the rest of the competition behind. The oldest 100-mile trail run in the U.S., the historic course starts in Squaw Valley, California and runs west to Auburn, traversing the trans-Sierra portion of the Western States Trail, which stretches from Salt Lake City, Utah to Sacramento.

The footpath was long ago trodden by the Paiute and Washoe peoples and later, in the middle to late 1800s, by the enterprising gold rush prospectors as a connection between the bustling gold camps of California and the booming silver mines of Nevada. Each June, runners climb more than 18,000 feet (5,486 meters) and descend 23,000 feet (7,010 meters) on these rugged trails over mountain passes, river crossings, and remote wilderness. One of the most competitive 100-mile races on the planet, it's no easy feat to even claim a spot at the prestigious start line.

As Olson navigated the final 20 miles of the course that late summer day in 2012, he experienced an intense focus and fluidity of movement, often referred to as "flow." Despite the long day, his aching legs and weary mind, his body traveled almost mystically through space, navigating each step with precision as he moved closer to the finish line in Auburn. "I was possessed by the trail," he wrote.

With just 7 miles to go, he stopped at an aid station and filled his hand-held bottle with Sierra Mist one last time and took off toward the finish in hopes of maintaining his lead. His physical pain was intense and he knew his muscles might seize up at any moment as he descended into the American River Canyon before arriving at the imposing No Hands Bridge. The structure looms 150 feet (45 meters) over the American River, which flows from the Sierra Nevada mountain range to its confluence with the Sacramento River.

As Olson pounded over the bridge that evening, he smiled to himself. "This is actually happening," he thought. "I'm going to win Western States." He navigated the final mile in an intense present-moment euphoria. The air buzzed with excitement. He felt out-of-body and electrified with awe and gratitude. The soft, late-day summer sun warmed him as it set in the mountains. Shirtless and sporting a healthy tan, Olson entered the Placer High School stadium and ran the final 300 meters on the track as he high-fived cheering fans standing on the in-field. His dirty and sweat-soaked blonde hair bounced at his shoulders as he strode across the finish line in a time of 14 hours, 46 minutes and 44 seconds, more than 20 minutes faster than anyone had ever run the race in its 36-year history.

Olson was welcomed on the track by his wife, Krista. They embraced before he leaned over to kiss her belly, pregnant with their first child. This was not only a major breakthrough in the ultrarunner's career, but also his life. Things hadn't always been this luminous for Olson. His story is one that shows that sometimes we have to hit rock bottom before we make the choice to wake up, climb out of the canyon of despair, one step at a time, across the old bridge, and toward something better.

Growing up in North Central Wisconsin's Tomorrow Valley, Olson logged many miles as a youngster through the corn and soybean fields near his home in the small village of Amherst. In high school, he joined the cross-country team to get in shape for basketball. He was a good runner, but after fleeing the nest for college, he stopped. Inertia took hold. A backward slide began. And he got lost.

Bad choices and destructive detours led Olson to drop out of college and spiral down the path of drugs and alcohol. He gained weight, got depressed, and eventually ended up in jail with a drug conviction. Hard-core drugs made life feel like it wasn't worth living, but he also worried he couldn't live without the chemicals.

He returned to running in 2006, when he was on probation for the drug conviction, in an attempt to detox his body and mind. On his road to sobriety, the opportunity to coach cross-country and track at his old high school in Wisconsin arose. This was a turning point for him. He rediscovered a joy of the sport through the eyes of the kids he coached. Soon he found himself running down the same rural backroads he once drove getting high and blaring loud music. His lungs burned and his legs resisted, but somehow it didn't hurt as bad as the lowest moments of his former life.

He went back to college, met his future wife, and kept on running. After he graduated, the couple headed west to Ashland, Oregon, a community of about 20,000 in the foothills of the scenic Siskiyou and Cascade ranges just north of the California border. He took to the natural beauty of the trails and eventually fell in with a new kind of crowd. Instead of drug dealers and addicts, he found kinship with a tribe of accomplished trail runners who lived and trained in the area.

***

I first met Olson just outside San Francisco on a press trip in 2013, about a year and a half after his big win at Western States, a race he won again that next year. I joined a group of writers and professional runners for breakfast at a sunny café in Mill Valley. Over coffee and eggs, Olson told me about his young son and the adventures he enjoyed with his wife as they traveled and he raced around the globe. Interestingly, it wasn't his training or future races he focused on, but rather, his family. There was a serene intensity about him and a sense of yogic philosophy humming in the background of his sentiments.

Olson's shift from addict to awakening fully eclipsed in 2009 when he was first introduced to mindfulness and the idea of "living in the now." The synergy between body and mind just

Whether you're training or racing, mindful awareness can reveal a more joyful running experience.

made sense to him as he traversed the mountain trails near his home in Ashland. He began observing the ever-changing nature of his breath and paying attention to how his body moved, focusing in on specific muscles, tendons, ligaments, and bones and how they all worked together to propel him forward.

"I noticed the more I practiced mindfulness and meditation, the more my runs would just click and flow," he told me. "I found that as I let go of any expectations and just appreciated the moment, the more focused and aware I was."

It was also around that time when he entered his first ultra race, a 50-kilometer event at which he came in sixth. The term "transformation" sounds trite, but that's the best way to describe what happened next. As Olson ran more miles and committed to serious mindfulness training, his life shifted. Not only did he begin his ascent to the top ranks of the professional ultrarunning world, he became increasingly content and more absorbed in the delights of everyday life in a way he'd never experienced before. There was something about this simple mindful running practice that changed the way he moved through the world. He explained:

"It's about being in the present moment on a run, connecting with your breath and your senses and enjoying movement not based on results, times or feelings. I focus on my breath and the rising and falling of my body and let thoughts, feelings and emotions arise, but I don't try to get rid of them. I stay curious and practice being at ease with them. It's as simple as that."

Today, Olson continues to compete in the upper echelons of ultra mountain running. When he's not on the move, he leads mindful running retreats where he shares the good word of present-moment awareness with other runners. He emphasized one important point to me: "Bringing mindfulness into anything you're passionate about ignites your overall enjoyment of the whole experience. You become more skilled by becoming engaged in and focused on what you're doing in the moment. The more you enjoy running, the better you are."

The Miracle of Neuroplasticity

While Olson's exploits of endurance are extreme, it turns out his experience isn't wholly unique. In addition to likely changing the very structure of his brain to support the sporting skill, his mindful approach served to boost his overall mental and emotional wellness. What's more, it has the potential to do the same for you.

Forging new neural pathways (the highways on which thoughts travel throughout the brain), mindful running can decrease stress, boost mood, and improve focus and concentration. Whether that means enhancing your training or influencing more significant aspects of your life, such as recovering from addiction and depression like in Olson's case, or changing the way you respond to the jerk who cuts you off in traffic, helping you develop greater patience for your child during a meltdown, or simply improving your focus and creativity at work, we can all benefit from the combined power of mindfulness and running as we move toward a more satisfied and successful existence.

How is this possible? In a word, "neuroplasticity."

"Neuroplasticity is the brain's ability to change in a long-lasting fashion," Fadel Zeidan told me. An assistant professor of neurobiology and anatomy at Wake Forest School of Medicine, he studies the unique ways mindfulness meditation affects the brain. From virtuoso violinists to jugglers to London taxi drivers, research has revealed that the form and function of the brain can be altered with certain training protocols.

Researchers at the Institute of Biomedical Sciences at Federal University of Rio de Janeiro estimate that there are somewhere around 86 billion neurons and hundreds of trillions of synapses firing, changing, and reorganizing into complex networks within our brains. The science of neuroplasticity demonstrates that the activities we engage in and the ways we think and emote all have the potential to influence those networks and change our brains, similar to the way that traditional exercise has long been known to transform our bodies. Commit to a regular regimen of bicep curls and those guns will grow; respond to challenges in life with an attitude of positivity, acceptance, and resilience and certain pathways in the brain are reinforced and new networks sprout.

You've probably heard the phrase "neurons that fire together wire together." It's the well-known abridged description of famed Canadian psychologist Donald Hebb's theory that when certain neurons in the brain fire at the same time, they become associated. Over time and repetition, our brains adapt to a new skill, pathways are strengthened, and the actions and responses become second nature.

The discovery of the "plastic" nature of the brain is particularly exciting because it was once thought that after early adulthood, the brain's neural conduits were set and that we couldn't modify the way we responded to things, no matter how hard we tried. So if you tend to dwell in anger, constantly criticize yourself, or default to impatience and frustration, experts said you were stuck. Imagine if, at a certain age, we had to resign to the fact that our physical fitness couldn't improve or that we could no longer hope to lose that extra weight around the midsection. That's what scientists long believed about the brain. What neuroplasticity research is teaching us is that with the proper training, we can effectively rewire our brains.

Mindful Movement for Brain-Body Fitness

So why do running and mindfulness make such a powerful combination in terms of brain training and mental fitness? As it turns out, scores of studies demonstrate that aerobic exercise not only promotes neuroplasticity by building new connections between neurons in the brain, it also triggers neurogenesis through the release of a protein called brain-derived neurotrophic factor (BDNF), which is commonly referred to as "Miracle-Gro for the brain." Feel like generating some new brain cells to boost memory and learning? Head out for a 30-minute run. Sustained aerobic exercise is one of the only things we know of that does this. For all the alternative benefits that other types of exercise offer, strength training can't produce loads of new brain cells the way running does; nor can high-intensity interval training. While stressful life experiences have been shown to decrease the production of neurons and connectivity in the brain, running helps generate almost twice as many new cells compared to sedentary controls in animal studies, and scientists believe it works the same way in humans.

In his essay "Walking," Henry David Thoreau observed the power locomotion has on the psyche, stating that when we move, "there will be so much more air and sunshine in our thoughts." Every runner knows what he meant by that. Running has a way of clearing out the mental cobwebs, improving cognitive clarity, and establishing a sunnier disposition. Among other benefits to brain health, aerobic exercise increases gray matter volume in multiple regions of the brain, which is thought to occur through the formation of new synapses between neurons that create more robust networks. This contributes to enhanced memory, emotional regulation, and overall cognitive function.

Running also initiates an endorphin rush, thereby blocking pain and triggering a sense of euphoria, as well as prompting the release of dopamine and serotonin, which additionally work to boost mood. That's not to mention the scores of well-known cardiovascular outcomes, reduction in cancer risk, weight loss, and increases in bone and muscle mass. That all sounds pretty great, so you may be wondering where mindfulness comes in. Isn't a clearer, more positive mental state, and a healthier body enough?

Infusing your training with awareness, intentionality, and purpose via mindfulness not only has the potential to amplify the already brain-boosting effects of aerobic exercise, it also comes with its own brand of rewards. The running list of empirical evidence is exhaustive. For instance, research conducted at Johns Hopkins University has demonstrated the efficacy of meditation in decreasing stress, anxiety, and depression. Other research published in the *Annals of Family Medicine* shows how mindfulness interventions have the power to reduce markers of inflammation and doctors at the Keck School of Medicine at the University of Southern California discovered that it can also fortify the immune system. Researchers at the Medical College of Georgia found that meditation lowered blood pressure in those who were at risk for developing hypertension and doctors at Stanford University Medical Center showed that it led to improvements in sleep for insomniacs. As you might expect when considering all the aforementioned outcomes, again and again researchers point to mindfulness as a major player in boosting overall quality of life in a wide variety of populations.

While the science is still in its infancy and we don't fully understand all the neurobiological mechanisms involved, mindfulness training also appears to influence the activity in and the architecture of the brain. Interestingly, research conducted by Judson Brewer revealed a number of fascinating things about the Default Mode Network (DMN), which brain imaging studies have demonstrated becomes activated when the mind wanders and ruminates over anxious or depressive thoughts. His research revealed that the DMN actually deactivates during mindfulness meditation.

As you'll learn in the coming pages, mind wandering can be associated with unhappiness and stress—many of us harbor a natural negativity bias—so when there is less activation in the DMN and more present-moment awareness, you can expect to experience a bump in contentment. Interestingly, when researchers from contemplative neuroscience pioneer Richard Davidson's lab at the University of Wisconsin-Madison looked at functional magnetic resonance imaging (fMRI) of the brains of practicing Buddhist monks, they found that their DMNs were deactivated at rest in a manner similar to other people actively meditating. This hints at the fact that, with lots of training, we may be able to teach our brains to remain in a present-moment state.

Further meditation research conducted through Davidson's Center for Healthy Minds has also found that the circuits in our brains that control emotions are linked to those that control thinking and cognition; they do not function independently of one another, as was once believed. That means that the thinking regions send signals via a complex network of circuits to the areas that breed feelings and emotions. By monitoring people's brain activity, Davidson has shown that, depending on the quality of communication between these regions, it either serves to ramp up feelings of depression, anxiety, fear, negativity, and anger or signals them to dissolve.

This suggests that mindfulness training can help you bring objective awareness to your thoughts and emotions, thereby teaching your "cognitive brain" to instruct your "emotional brain" to chill out. Indeed, it is the way we react to difficult thoughts and emotions that is often far more harmful than the cognitions and feelings themselves. You've probably heard of the fight/flight/freeze response. You start thinking about being unfairly slighted by someone and are soon caught up in a riptide of rumination, which, in turn, causes a physical response: Sweating, tense muscles, and increased heart rate.

Most of us are hardwired for vigilance. What mindfulness does is it dials you in to the present moment so you can observe thoughts and feelings and then respond objectively. In effect, it downgrades the power of your most primitive emotional responses, while putting higher order thought in the driver's seat.

It creates space in your mind for inquiry and allows for improved emotional regulation. As researchers from the Jaypee Institute of Information Technology in India observed after studying the effect mindfulness training had on well-being, people who are mindful more adeptly cope with challenging thoughts and feelings, thereby avoiding getting emotionally overwhelmed. The thinking goes that over time, even for those of us who are intensely set in our ways, mindfulness can actually influence the synaptic organization of your brain so you don't get so hung up on the negative and stressed by the ups and downs of life.

Adrienne Taren, a neuroscientist and mindfulness researcher at the University of Pittsburgh, offered me a nice analogy:

> *"Mindfulness gives you a flashlight and you have control over where you point that flashlight. You can direct your attention or flashlight away from panicky or ruminative thoughts and emotional responses and shine it somewhere more productive. It's not that those thoughts aren't there, you just learn to peacefully coexist by not shining the light on them."*

Zeidan, who utilizes fMRI in his research at Wake Forest to monitor how mindfulness meditation might change the brain, put it to me this way:

> *"Mindfulness meditation trains your mind and brain to stabilize attention and it increases your ability to regulate emotions by being in the present moment. Over time, in order to continuously facilitate those behaviors and types of experiences, the mind adapts to better stabilize them. What's happening is your personality becomes more present-centered, better able to focus and better able to regulate emotions as a function of a potentially more efficient brain."*

While it is difficult to study runners utilizing mindfulness on the run, all of the authorities on the subject with whom I spoke, from sports psychologists to neuroscientists to coaches, said that anecdotally, the two make a symbiotic pairing.

One of them was neuroscientist Leslie Sherlin. While he told me he often finds himself getting caught up in thinking about his next session with a client or the paperwork piling up on his desk at other times of the day, when he runs, he is able to settle into a rhythm and give himself over to the movement. Running, he told me, offers him a platform to simply practice being in the moment, unchained from the other stresses of life. "Mindfulness and running go together really well," he said. "The running movement naturally leads you toward a more mindful state, making it easier to fall into that awareness from a cognitive perspective. It allows me to observe smells, textures, colors, and what the air feels like as I pass through it, so I can really take it all in."

Tracey Shors, a neuroscientist at the Center for Collaborative Neuroscience at Rutgers University, also a runner, shares Sherlin's affinity for engaging in meditative aerobic exercise. As such, she was inspired to devise a study based on the knowledge that while running makes way for the birth of new brain cells, mindfulness might just be one of the best methods to keep them healthy.

To be sure, the survival of those new cells isn't guaranteed— in fact, nearly half of them will die within weeks of genesis. What they discovered with rats was that "effortful learning" and concentration on skill development over time helped neurons thrive. While they don't yet know exactly how it works in the human brain, Shors and her colleagues wanted to take this data and apply it to an intervention people could actually use, so she set out to identify an activity that required effortful learning.

"I was chatting with a friend of mine one day who suggested we try meditation because it is effortful and it always presents a new learning experience," she told me. "At first I thought that seemed a little too fluffy for me because I had this really unsophisticated and naïve view of what meditation was about, but when I finally decided to try it, I thought, 'Wow, this is definitely effortful.'"

To put it to the test, Shors and her colleagues paired mindfulness meditation with aerobic exercise. They dubbed it "MAP Training," short for "Mental and Physical Training", (maptrainmybrain.com) and instructed participants to do 20 minutes of sitting mindfulness meditation, 10 minutes of walking meditation, and 30 minutes of running. When utilized by a group of participants with major depressive disorder twice a week for eight weeks, they discovered a 40 percent reduction in depressive symptoms, a decrease in ruminative thoughts, and enhanced synchronicity of brain activity, which basically means it boosted brain function and contributed to a greater sense of well-being.

"Mindfulness meditation and aerobic exercise make a nice combination, even over and above what it might be doing to neurogenesis in the hippocampus. It's time efficient and seems to be satisfying to participants," added Shors, who continues to employ both mindfulness and aerobic exercise in her own daily routine.

Now that we've covered the way mindfulness can enhance well-being, you may be wondering how it might influence your running. Next, we will look at the ways greater awareness can boost enjoyment in your daily workouts and thereby influence performance.

Running for Joy

As she climbs in elevation, Mirna Valerio cruises past tumbling whitewater, serene lakes, and steep coves crawling with rhododendron. Ravens ride the rising air currents overhead as her feet make haste over the iron-rich, rust-tinged earth that is characteristic of the high country of northeastern Georgia where she lives and trains. At the summit, she is treated to 360-degree panoramic views of the rocky and rugged landscape below. She's breathing hard and her legs ache from the ascent, but it's hard not to love running in this setting. The beauty of this landscape is definitely not lost on Valerio.

A teacher, administrator, choir director and cross-country coach at a prep school in Rabun County, Georgia, she has gained recognition in the running world for shattering stereotypes. The 5-foot-7, 250-pound African American runner blogs about her adventures at *Fat Girl Running*—and those adventures are abundant, including nine marathons and nine ultramarathons. Her secret to success, she says, is simply being intentional about running and accepting who she is, which contributes to the joy she experiences in the humble act of putting one foot in front of the other.

While she reserves certain runs to turn over challenges in her mind and dream up creative solutions to problems, she spends most of her time engaged in the freedom of movement. "I'm always looking for beauty—that visual inspiration," she told me. "I experience the vibrant colors of fall and the snowy winter trail,

Mindfulness shifts the way you relate to your body, mind, and the world around you.

the landscape is always changing and I love how dynamic that makes my training."

Along with being present in her environment, she has developed a keen awareness of her body and mind. The key, she says, is simply expecting some level of physical discomfort. "I know at a certain point during a run it's going to be painful or I'll feel tired and sluggish. I go out there knowing it's going to become difficult. I totally accept that. It just comes with the territory."

While she's recognized for her positive attitude, she admits that her internal dialogue isn't always upbeat. Self-doubt and negativity also come with the territory—it's a matter of whether she chooses to entertain them. "I just let myself have those thoughts, I know they are there, but I also know they aren't true," she explained. "I'm never going to be elite. I run because I love running. I don't care what other people say, I know I'm a runner."

Valerio has already figured out what research studies are beginning to show: Being in tune with the present moment and accepting things as they are can play a major role in boosting joy and meaning in life. While advances in brain imaging over the last 15 years have inspired mountains of new research in the field of mind wandering, researchers long struggled to test it out in the real world.

Then in 2010, Matt Killingsworth, a doctoral student in psychology at Harvard University at the time, came up with an elegant way to leverage the ever-present nature of smartphones. To do so, he designed a smartphone app called "Track Your Happiness," which sent alerts to study participants to gather data on what they were thinking about and doing in particular moments.

The study found that people reported mind wandering a whopping 47 percent of the time. This is a stunning finding when you think about it. Most of us are frittering away nearly half of our waking hours lost in thought. The problem with this, Killingsworth suggests, is that when your mind wanders, it tends to generate worries, regrets, judgments, and to-do lists.

Killingsworth's research revealed that people are significantly happier when they are focused on the present than when their minds are wandering. Consider Valerio's description of running. She feels joy and contentment because she switches on and tunes in to the awesome nature of her experience. One 2015 study by Dutch researchers actually showed that mindfulness helps facilitate awareness of positive feelings and a parallel increase in exercise satisfaction by fostering an ability to tune in to the sights, sounds, and smells of a run with greater nuance.

"Mindfulness helps me really capture what I'm experiencing in the moment running outdoors," Rick Hecht told me, referring to his favorite running routes near his home on the east side of San Francisco Bay. The professor of medicine at the University of California, San Francisco, as well as an ultrarunner and mindfulness practitioner, Hecht continued, "Even when my body is tired or I'm feeling discomfort, I love being out running on this amazing network of trails right out my back door. It's part of what I do to balance the rest of my life and stay fit, as well as being part of my spiritual practice."

Being a mindful runner and associating with the physical, mental, emotional and experiential act of running means you not only reap the physiological benefits of aerobic exercise, but also a whole host of mental and emotional payoffs. For the more competitive-minded runners, whether it be in preparing for your first 5K or chasing a personal best in the marathon, mindfulness also happens to have the potential to improve performance by way of this increased enjoyment.

A Performance-Enhancing Mindset

"I consciously shifted my mental energy from dreading upcoming discomfort to simply recognizing that pain will always appear in slight variations of itself and I should try

to greet it politely. When I am sad, even though it's a quieter pain than in a race, I still feel it physically, like a Jenga-block push to the heart. As when I am running, I try to stay calm and be mentally OK with sadness, anger or any emotion I know is normal every once in a while."

As you might expect based on her eloquent words, 10,000-meter Olympian Alexi Pappas' talent reaches far beyond the track. A renaissance woman of sorts, she's also a poet, writer, actor, and filmmaker. That is all on top of the fact that in 2016 she was one of the fastest U.S. women in both the 5,000 and 10,000 meters. While she lives and trains in Eugene, Oregon, she is of Greek descent, which is how she wound up representing Greece at the 2016 Olympics. She was the first Greek woman to run the 10,000 meters at the Games and her time was a Greek national record.

Beyond her running success, it is Pappas' personal brand of expressive flair that makes her so beloved among her fans. The 26-year-old's signature top-bun hairstyle has its own Twitter account, she frequently talks about her sponsorship with a local butcher shop that offers her a weekly ration of steak, and she co-wrote, co-directed, and starred as Olympic-hopeful Plumb Marigold in her feature-length movie *Tracktown*, which premiered at the 2016 Los Angeles Film Festival and starred a couple *Saturday Night Live* alums.

While some may suggest that she is spreading herself too thin, Pappas insists that the passionate pursuit of multiple paths helps her achieve greater balance. All are mutually exclusive—her running profits from her creative endeavors and vice versa. Her key to juggling it all? She points to mindfulness, explaining that she doesn't waste time getting caught up in the past or future or the push and pull of thoughts, emotions, and expectations.

Having practiced mindfulness meditation and applied it to her running for years, it has become deeply ingrained in her identity and in the ways she expresses herself through writing, running, and acting. When I asked her recently how mindfulness comes in handy in high stakes competition, she told me:

> *"During races I get in the zone by thinking about the word 'stay.' Especially with longer races, which are more about attrition than anything else, it's often the person who hangs in the longest who finishes in the front. If I keep saying the word 'stay' to myself, it keeps me calm and focused."*

* * *

Traditional sports psychology emphasizes enhancing performance outcomes via psychological skills training (PST), which includes strategies like goal setting, visualization, self-talk, and thought-stopping. While these are all effective in certain situations, and most athletes have relied on them at one time or another, they require you to muster up control over thoughts, emotions, physical sensations, and experiences.

Interestingly, research tells us that the more we try not to think about something, the more we are likely to do so. Daniel Wegner, a social psychology professor at Harvard University at the forefront of thought suppression research, called this the "ironic process theory" or the "white bear problem." The latter comes from Fyodor Dostoevsky's 1863 account of his travels through Western Europe, during which he wrote, "Try to pose for yourself this task: not to think of a polar bear, and you will see that the cursed thing will come to mind every minute." Put simply, the theory posits that an internal battle often erupts when we try to resist or force certain thoughts.

In race-car driving, it is often said that a driver's car will follow their gaze. So if you have your eyes set on a crash barrier going around a turn at over 100 miles per hour, it's likely you'll end up driving right into it. In downhill skiing, it is generally advised to focus on the space between the trees as you scan the terrain, rather than the trees themselves if you hope to avoid smacking into one. In the same way, when we try to tell ourselves to stop thinking about, for instance, how much our legs hurt running up a hill, and replace those thoughts with more chipper cognitions, we ironically think of the pain even more.

This is exactly what neuroscientist Adrienne Taren has experienced in her own training. A runner and triathlete, she's no stranger to the wide spectrum of negative thoughts that often enter the cognitive landscape in the midst of competition. In particular, after a bad bike crash, she found that she was having trouble subduing overwhelming feelings of panic and anxiety every time she got in the saddle. She told me:

> *"There are all these psych studies that show that trying to suppress negative thoughts during exercise actually worsens performance. That was a big ah-ha moment for me with mindfulness because that's exactly what I've experienced. When I was able to first just sit with the negative and not have an emotional response to it, then I could direct myself away from it."*

In 2015, I had a similar experience with the swim portion of Ironman Wisconsin. One of a handful of Ironman events that involves a mass start—3,000 athletes gingerly enter the waters of Lake Monona together and tread in place until the start canon fires. In a split second, the surface of the lake goes from calm and glassy to something more akin to a massive washing machine churning green water and neoprene-covered arms and legs. Every time I tried to get my body horizontal to swim forward, someone behind me would reach their arm out to stroke and inadvertently drag my legs back down underwater. Or I'd get in a rhythm for a moment and an athlete much larger than myself would aggressively swim right over the top of me or elbow me in the face and knock my goggles off.

I desperately gasped for air and choked on lake water. "Don't panic! How am I ever going to get through this? Don't panic!" I said to myself on the verge of panic. Fortunately, a mindful voice of reason then spoke up: "This situation already sucks and you're starting to feel really anxious." In the chaotic scene, I was already having trouble getting a clean breath and I knew if I expended more energy trying to deny feelings of panic, I'd start hyperventilating and be in real trouble. I said to myself: "You're getting kicked in the face and pushed under the water, but you're still moving forward. It's okay to feel anxious, that's normal. Just take this one stroke at a time."

That simple internal dialogue was enough to tune me back in to the moment with mindful awareness at a time when I was at risk of getting carried away by reactive emotions. By just focusing on what was directly in front of me, taking that next stroke, and riding the waves of mayhem, I was able to calm myself down and avoid making a difficult situation more challenging than it already was.

* * *

Mindfulness training can serve as a complement to conventional psychological skills training or as an alternative. Runners often needlessly waste time and energy denying and resisting physical sensations, thoughts, and emotions, frantically grasping for the right psychological tool to address the situation. It's akin to indiscriminately hammering away with a blunt instrument when poise and precision are called for. What mindfulness does is it trains you to tune into the running experience so you can better judge when it is best to deploy specific psychological strategies. For instance, for a runner who has a tendency to choke under pressure, mindfulness might help them identify a lack of confidence as the root of the problem. As such, you may decide that visualization is the most useful instrument to combat this anxiety.

Additionally, mindfulness can be used as an alternative to some of these conventional tools. Rather than trying to replace negative self-talk with more positive cognitions, for example, a runner might decide to mindfully focus in on the thought until it dissipates. It's somewhat similar to when a massage therapist applies firm pressure to a knot in a muscle; it is initially uncomfortable, but eventually the focused attention allows the knot to release and melt away.

Mindfulness changes the way you relate to your experiences. It trains you to notice and accept internal states and external realities without getting caught up trying to steer your experience in a specific direction. As psychologist Susan David explains in her book *Emotional Agility*, there's a lot to be learned from life's greatest challenges "once we stop trying to smother them with positive affirmations or rationalizations."

For many athletes, the process of noticing, but not attaching to thoughts and feelings, can defuse a normally charged situation by removing the pressure to control, regulate, resist, deny, or defy. When we embrace mindfulness and stop trying to change things through sheer force of will, when we let go, we set ourselves up for those goals to finally be realized via greater ease of mind, fluidity of movement, and improved decision-making.

To be sure, there are studies that back up this idea. Researchers at The Catholic University of America in Washington D.C. who administered the Mindful Sport Performance Enhancement (MSPE) program to runners hypothesize that mindfulness may aid running performance because it guides athletes to focus in on the most relevant of data in the moment. In learning to accept the fatigue, boredom, and discomfort in a nonjudgmental way, you become less self-critical and better able to simply focus on the task at hand.

Of course, this doesn't mean that you sit back and always accept feelings, thoughts, and emotions without action. Mindfulness simply aids you in becoming more aware so you can rationally decide if a response is necessary. Sherlin explained this idea to me, saying that mindfulness "helps an athlete clue in to how their brain is behaving and realize when they aren't being purposeful in their actions. It's always this ability to zero in on the moment they are in, relax, and feel it in this rich way."

This also highlights the way mindfulness hones body awareness. "When I have a peaceful, tuned-in mind, I am better able to listen to my body," Pappas said. Research even suggests that a distracted mindset can potentially increase your chances of getting injured. Some experts believe that, as a result of the repetitive nature of the sport, runners are more likely to get lulled into complacency and let their minds wander, thereby causing us to miss vital physiological red flags.

As you will see in the subsequent chapters, accepting some level of physical discomfort through mindful running will not only allow you to achieve more than you thought possible, you'll also find that pain and fatigue are often dictated by the mind more than the body. Mindfulness teaches you to coexist with a certain amount of discomfort, whether it be mental, physical, or emotional, which leads to a release of tension and greater fluidity of movement. And as I will explain, mindfulness sets the stage to enter the flow state by emphasizing present-moment awareness of the process of training over any one objective or ambition. But let us not get ahead of ourselves. First, we must learn how to get motivated to take those first mindful steps.

Chapter 2

GETTING STARTED: BUILDING A FOUNDATION OF AUTHENTICITY

"If you had told me I was going to set world or American records, I would have laughed. When you're heavy and depressed, you're just exhausted every day, so when you come home, you don't want to do anything. You're already tired, so why would you want to go workout? But once you start running, you actually have more energy and that energy and happiness gradually increase simultaneously. For me, running 100 miles was like losing weight. I just decided I was done being fat, tired, and depressed. In the same way, going into my first 100-mile race, I had this attitude that I was going to finish that thing come hell or high water."

As evidenced by her above comments to me in the summer of 2016, American ultrarunning champion Traci Falbo has lived at both ends of the spectrum. At the age of 31, she found herself worn out, depressed, and 80 pounds overweight. She hadn't always been that way. In fact, she ran cross-country in high school and college, but the passage of time, two children, and marital troubles all contributed to the increasing numbers on the scale. She knew she was depressed because she was overweight and overweight because she was depressed—a frustrating cycle in which many people find themselves. Yet, in March 2003, against all odds, she decided she needed to make a change.

The full-time pediatric physical therapist started with 5 a.m. wake-up calls every morning to meet a friend at the gym and hit the treadmills. In the beginning it was a slow, miserable slog. Gradually, however, she saw a reduction in both her weight and her feelings of despair. By the end of summer, 15 pounds had come off and she discovered that instead of making her more exhausted, running actually boosted her energy levels and drive. For the first time in a while, a ray of hope for the future broke through. A year out from starting her gym routine, she had lost nearly 80 pounds, and in December 2004 she logged an impressive 3 hour 32 minute finish at the Rocket City Marathon in Huntsville, Alabama.

With the benefit of momentum, she wasn't about to stop there. Next came ambitions to join the 50 States Club by running a marathon in every U.S. state. The following season, she logged her first 100-mile race at the Cajun Coyote in Ville Platte, Louisiana. Not only did she finish, she won.

"At that point I realized that I might not be fast at shorter distances, but I could do the long distances really well," she told me for a 2016 piece for *Competitor* magazine. "I'm stubborn and determined and don't quit easily."

Indeed, in subsequent years, she's been a two-time member of the U.S. 24-hour ultrarunning team, held the American record in the 100-mile trail event, and broken the American 48-hour and world 48-hour indoor track records (running a whopping 242.093 miles/389.610 km in that time).

Falbo's story may sound unique, but I believe that her process-oriented approach is accessible to just about anyone. She didn't start out 80 pounds overweight with aspirations to be an elite ultra-distance runner. She would have surely scoffed at any hint of that notion at the time. Instead, she set her sights on simply being a happier, healthier person. On the road toward reaching those objectives, she discovered that with each pound lost, her motivation mounted. Becoming a decorated athlete was simply a by-product of the process.

Mindful Motivation

Do you take on new goals and projects with gusto, only to lose steam soon after? Do you feel you could be more successful if you were more driven? Do you find yourself so overwhelmed by life's responsibilities that you can't imagine taking on another activity? From eating your vegetables, to going to bed earlier, to subscribing to a new workout plan, we've all experienced going from inspired to indifferent in just a matter of days. To be sure, researchers in the UK who monitored adherence to exercise found that upward of 50 percent of people quit within six months of starting.

Physicians and researchers have long worked to crack the code on how to best establish healthy habits. One 2009 study published in the *European Journal of Social Psychology* found that it takes an average of 66 days of consistently executing a particular task for it to become ingrained in your daily life—with that said, some people only required 18 days, while others needed up to 254 days, so there is quite a range. Of course it's okay to slip up here and there, but more often than not you have to stay on track for an average of two months to make it habitual.

The reason it's important to turn running into a habit, whether that means getting out two days a week or six, is that if you don't set a clear path for when, where, why, and how you're going to run, it's likely you won't, at least not regularly enough to make it productive. That may be due to something called "decision fatigue," a term coined by social psychologist Roy F. Baumeister at Florida State University, which basically posits that we only have a finite amount of energy to lend to self-control. Once that runs out, willpower evaporates and we become unmotivated to make certain decisions. When running becomes a predictable part of your routine, however, it gets easier to persuade yourself to get out the door because it eliminates the energy-zapping process of decision-making.

As such, it is vital to adopt what Carol Dweck, a psychologist and author of *Mindset: The New Psychology of Success*, calls a "growth mindset." This is basically the belief that you are capable of developing new skills—that you can continuously achieve greater levels of personal growth if you put forth the effort. In contrast, a "fixed mindset" is one that assumes your skills are set in stone and can't be enhanced, no matter how hard you try. It's that inner narrator that tells you you're crazy for signing up for that 5K or having ambitions to run a personal best. Conversely, a growth mindset is one that urges you to take the necessary actions to achieve continued development.

"A growth mindset indicates that we are on this journey for mastery and self-improvement, which means every single situation in sport or life has something to teach us," sports psychologist, runner, and Ironman triathlete Gloria Petruzzelli told me. "While growth and improvement doesn't always feel good, mindfulness reminds us that pain and discomfort are temporary and something wonderful can grow from them."

Exercise 2.1: Think of a time when you were highly motivated. It could be a memory of just about anything—training for a race, studying for an exam, working on a home improvement project. Come up with five adjectives that describe the way that felt and write them down in your training journal. Next, come up with three reasons why that activity was important to you.

When we are walking through life in a state of constant distraction, which as I mentioned is around 47 percent of the time for most of us, we often don't notice our destructive and unhealthy habits, like planting ourselves on the sofa for five hours after work every day instead of going for a run. When you mindfully tune in, you likely realize, "Wow, this doesn't feel very good," which can be

Over time and training, running with mindful awareness becomes second nature.

a great catalyst for change. Mindfulness positions you to discern what is productive and what is unproductive.

So how do you harness the motivation necessary to turn running into a habit, especially in those first 66 days when decision fatigue may be weighing you down? In his book, *The Craving Mind*, Judson Brewer introduces a simple formula to explain how both good and bad habits are formed: "Trigger. Behavior. Reward." So for instance, he explained to me that stress could be the trigger, eating a cupcake the behavior, and experiencing satisfaction from the sugar rush the reward. The problem is that we frequently rely on extrinsic rewards like cupcakes to deal with many of our thoughts and emotions. Those types of rewards are only satisfying in the short term and they often prove to be harmful over time.

"What if instead we could build rewards based on intrinsic motivators?" Brewer posited to me. An intrinsically motivating activity is one that you enjoy for its own sake. Curiosity is key to this process, he says, because that in and of itself is inherently rewarding. He used this example: You're on a run and you begin to feel stressed (trigger), you get curious about what that stress feels like—maybe you notice your shoulders are tense or your jaw is clenched (behavior), so you let go and relax into the run (reward). "You get this intrinsic reward from not only the feeling of curiosity, but also the joy of letting go and not getting caught up in the stress," he explained.

Philosophy, literature, and religion are full of accounts about the importance of shedding our long-held paradigms and viewing experiences with fresh eyes. Marcel Proust's ponderings are often aptly paraphrased this way: "The real voyage of discovery consists not in seeking new landscapes, but in having new eyes."

Similarly, in renowned psychoanalyst David Shainberg's contemplations on the meditative nature of running, he wrote:

"Each day the run has a different context. The weather is different, the day before was different, the distance is different ... Although my body appears to be the same as yesterday, it is in fact quite different and its difference partakes of the almost infinite number of variations in this new day's run."

The intrinsic reward of mindful curiosity can feed your motivation to run. In fact, a 2016 study by French researchers found an association between the enhanced awareness achieved through mindfulness and intrinsic motivation to exercise more. When I was working on a story about the link between running enjoyment and motivation for *Runner's World* magazine a few years ago, sports psychologist and sub-three-hour marathoner Jim Taylor told me, "When you get a fundamental enjoyment from just being out there running, it keeps you going."

Moment-to-moment awareness has a way of putting greater emphasis on the process of training, contributing to an enthusiasm for the day-in and day-out effort required. Other studies have shown that people who report being mindful during exercise are also more satisfied with their workouts, which is one of the major reasons we stick with a training regimen. University of Quebec psychology professor Robert J. Vallerand calls this "harmonious passion," which is characterized by the drive to engage in the daily work certain activities require simply because you take joy in the process.

In summing up Aristotle's thinking on the subject, historian and philosopher Will Durant wrote, "We are what we repeatedly do. Excellence, then, is not an act, but a habit." As research into neuroplasticity and exercise physiology has shown, we harbor the power to change our bodies and brains through the activities we engage in and the thoughts we have. Whether you decide to sit in front of the television all day letting your brain do as it pleases, or you adopt a more mindful mindset and head out for a run, the ruts of those well-worn paths get more and more entrenched in your modus operandi.

Setting True North Goals

The foundation of your mindful running routine should be rooted in an overarching intention you set for training. It is what will kick you in the butt and motivate you to lace up and get out the door, even on the days you'd prefer to laze around.

The objectives you set forth for your mindful running routine will diverge from more conventional, results-oriented goals. While pie-in-the-sky aspirations provide a major target or finish line to strive for, these types of goals can be ambitious to the point of being defeating. As a recent Harvard Business School report entitled "Goals Gone Wild" suggests, narrowly focused, results-driven goals actually reduce intrinsic motivation in many cases.

"What mindfulness teaches us is to focus on the process of getting there. When we are overly focused on achievement, it detracts from the experience and can work against us, thereby making it harder to fulfill certain goals," explained Elinor Fish, the founder of Run Wild Retreats, a company that organizes mindful running excursions all over the globe.

What if instead of getting caught up obsessing over results-oriented goals, we focused more on the process of logging mindful miles, as Fish suggests? Benoît Lecomte, the French-born long-distance swimmer who in 1998 became the first to swim 3,716 miles (5,980 km) across the Atlantic Ocean without a kickboard, once said in a National Public Radio interview: "I never jump into the water thinking about the entire ocean, I just cut it into small pieces. When I am in the middle of the ocean, I think about being in a pool and the pool moves with me."

In yoga they refer to this as "setting an intention," which is the method of establishing an objective for practice that is process-oriented and reaches beyond the mat. Intentions are concerned with the greater purpose behind why you're doing what you're doing and the day-to-day work it takes to pursue that path. In the context of mindful running, I like to call these "True North Goals."

Exercise 2.2: If you had three words to describe yourself, what would they be? Contemplate how those things shape your identity.

***

Some of my first attempts at integrating mindfulness into my running routine occurred in college on the shrouded forest trails that snaked along the banks of the serene Lake Sagatagan in bucolic Collegeville, Minnesota. My destination was always the Stella Maris Chapel, an old abandoned sanctuary built deep in the woods by Benedictine monks in 1872.

The name "Stella Maris" means "Star of the Sea," another name for Polaris or the North Star. The North Star has long been used by navigators and astronomers to guide the way to true north

Mindful running emphasizes long-term growth and development over short-term ambitions.

without high-tech navigational tools or even a compass. Always pointing toward the north celestial pole, this lodestar can help light the way whether you're bushwhacking through the deep wilderness or sailing on the open seas. Since the North Star hangs nearly right above Earth's northern axis, like a stellar hub of a bicycle wheel, it remains in the same spot in the northern sky while all other stars spin around it.

A True North Goal serves as the North Star for your mindful running practice and for living at large. Psychologist Susan David writes in her book, *Emotional Agility*, "Your core values provide the compass that keeps you moving in the right direction." Your True North Goal is more meaningful than those related to pace, pounds, or mileage. Rather, this objective lights the way toward self-improvement and greater contentment by emphasizing process over results. Faster times and a healthier body just happen often to be by-products of this more authentic approach to fitness. Just as mindfulness meditation teaches that you can always come back to your breath in moments of anxiety, sadness, anger, fear, or confusion, so can you always return to true north for a way forward. Not sure where to start in determining your True North Goal?

Ask yourself the following questions:

- What matters to me most in life?
- What makes me happiest?
- What would I most like to let go of?
- How would I describe my best self?
- What do I feel grateful for?

Exercise 2.3: After pondering these questions for a few minutes, grab your training journal and write down all the things that come to mind when considering your True North Goals for your mindful running practice. Treat this as a free-form writing exercise. Don't toil over thoughts for too long, you can revise these later—just write down everything that comes to mind.

Here are a few examples of True North Goals for mindful running:

- Learn to find more joy in running and everyday life.
- Discover greater emotional balance.
- Gain a better understanding of my thoughts and emotions.
- Learn to listen to my body and take better care of it.
- Find focus and calm.
- Become more at ease in my own skin.

* * *

Utah-based runner Blu Robinson's story perfectly illustrates this process. For a 2016 *Competitor* magazine story, I interviewed the 40-year-old mental health counselor and founder of Addict II Athlete, a non profit that combines running and therapy to help people with various addictions. Today, the marathon and ultramarathon runner is the image of health, but it wasn't always that way. He grew up in poverty, dropped out of high school, and fell in with the wrong crowd early in life. By the time he reached adulthood, he was depressed and battling a serious drug and alcohol addiction.

It was through discovering first mountain biking and then running that he turned things around. These activities took the place of the substances he had long been putting into his body. As he trained by foot and bike, he found meaning in his miles and his identity shifted from addict to endurance athlete. His training wasn't about physical strength or speed, although those were welcome derivatives, but rather he sought greater wellness and self-betterment. His True North Goal was to lead a healthier, more authentic life mentally, emotionally, physically, and spiritually.

Following his North Star, he eventually went back to school to get his high school diploma and later a degree in counseling. He also fell in love with a woman whose father urged him to run his first marathon. He stepped up to that challenge and went far beyond it, now running races as long as 100 miles. He told me:

> *"As I was struggling during that first marathon, as bad as I was hurting, it didn't even compare to the pain I felt when my parents got divorced, or when we went hungry at night because we were so poor, or when I was totally alone in my addiction. With running, I knew I could push through it — that I had trained for this and could finish."*

Then, even more impressive, he continues to work to pay it forward by sharing the power of running with others. To date he's helped thousands of addicts and their families chart their own courses toward healthier living.

As Robinson's story demonstrates, while your True North Goal serves as your North Star or guiding principle for your training, that doesn't mean that you can't have other, more performance-oriented objectives you want to chase as well; there are plenty of stars in the sky. The main difference is that these stars aren't as bright and they are constantly in motion, rotating as part of a greater celestial sphere. These are the goals related to losing weight, running a certain distance, or setting a personal best time.

Setting S.M.A.R.T. Goals

While True North Goals remain constant despite changing circumstances, these objectives may need to be adjusted throughout your training. Perhaps an injury sidelines you for several weeks and you have to rethink your race calendar. On the flip side, maybe you're seeing more progress in your weight-loss journey, so you need to raise the bar. The key to setting these results-driven goals is to apply the principles of mindfulness so you know when to tweak them.

An approach taken from the world of business, I guide the athletes I coach to choose S.M.A.R.T. goals, which stands for Specific, Measurable, Achievable, Realistic, and Time-bound.

- **Specific** Set up a time and a place for your goals to be achieved. Signing up for a race or identifying an event for which you want to lose weight are good examples.
- **Measurable** Instead of setting a nebulous goal, like "I want to be a faster runner," go into a bit more detail. It could be, "I want to run a two-minute PR in the half marathon" or "I want to lose 10 pounds for my wedding in August."
- **Achievable** Choose a goal that pushes you, but isn't totally out of your reach.
- **Relevant** Your goals should sprout from your own personal ambitions, not just something your running buddy wants to do.
- **Time-bound** Keep your training on a timeline. If you signed up for a race, this takes care of keeping it time-bound.

As I previously mentioned, I have a history of getting too fixated on S.M.A.R.T. goals. When I learned to embrace process over results, personal growth over the achievement of one particular race goal, and mindfulness over mindlessness, I discovered better and happier running. Now when I encounter setbacks in achieving my S.M.A.R.T. goals, like in the case of a disappointing race, it doesn't feel so calamitous. While these goals sometimes move and change, my True North always remains.

Exercise 2.4: While you don't need to set S.M.A.R.T. goals, if you have some in mind, write them down in your training journal. If you have more than one, label them "a," "b," "c" and so forth in order of importance. For instance, your "a" goal could be to run a personal best time in the 5K and your "b" goal could be to finish under a specific time.

Mindful Running Rules of Engagement

In journalism, we often fall back on a series of questions known as the "Five Ws and one H" or "5W1H" in order to gather material and problem-solve. Prior to entering *focus-fathom-flow* mode, the following 5W1H is a list of logistical considerations to keep in mind at the outset of your mindful running practice.

- **What** Mindful running is defined as running with a wide open, present-moment awareness of physical sensations, cognitions, and emotions.
- **Who** Mindfulness is for every runner. Whether you're jogging a few miles a week for fitness, tackling your first 5K, looking to break five hours in the marathon, or racing in the upper levels of the sport, mindful running has something to offer. Early on, learning to be a more mindful runner is usually best accomplished running on your own. Many runners will find that noticing thoughts, feelings, and physical sensations is more challenging than expected, so allowing yourself the time and space to adopt this new mindset without distraction is

important. As those new neural pathways are forged, however, mindfulness becomes a way of running and life. As a result, it is a great state of mind to adopt when running with others and can contribute to flow of conversation and connection. Some of my best and most vivid running memories come from running with my husband when we first started dating. Indeed, present-moment awareness will improve the quality of your interactions with your spouse, running buddies, or teammates and lead to a shared sense of purpose.

- **Where** Tuning in to your mind, body, and environment can be done just about anywhere. First and foremost, it is important always to attend to your personal safety, whether it be taking precautions in high-traffic areas or avoiding secluded trails. While most runners will find running outside in nature with few distractions to be most conducive to achieving a mindful state—there is plenty of research that shows its positive influence on health—urban settings and tracks are certainly not off-limits. It is also possible to run with mindfulness on a treadmill. In fact, one of the big reasons that studio treadmill classes are taking off is because people of different paces can run together, which is a wonderful training ground for engaging in relational mindfulness.
- **When** Mindfulness is something you can call upon on easy jogs, hard workouts, long runs, and in races. In all these scenarios, it can play an important role in tuning you in to the present moment to help you regulate pace, effort, and mental and physical wellness. In races, being in the moment is particularly vital to set the stage to enter flow, which is where peak performance lives.
- **Why** By its nature, mindfulness helps us cultivate authenticity. We become freer, more flexible, and willing to welcome each new moment as it arises. This peace of mind and ease of living allows us to see the world, the people around us, and

ourselves with greater clarity. Patience, curiosity, and focus shift to the top of the compass. Cultivating this mindset through running, in turn, leads to greater satisfaction and performance in training.

- **How** We all love our gadgets. Mindful running simply calls gearheads and tech hounds to be aware and attentive of their utilization of them. Feel free to use your newfangled GPS watch, heart-rate monitor, and fancy smartphone apps. You can even run with music if you must. The key is not to let any of these things get in the way of tuning in to the present moment and engaging in the act of forward motion. Every brain functions differently—what one person finds distracting, another discovers it helps them focus and relax. Simply be aware of how your body and mind respond to your use of technology and determine if it's productive or unproductive as you work to achieve a more mindful state. If you've never run without these accessories, I urge you to give it a shot.

Essential Gear: There is one piece of low-tech gear, besides running shoes, I suggest getting your hands on: a training journal. Although not required, it'll come in handy if you're interested in trying the various exercises as you work through this book.

It doesn't matter if you're fast or slow, a veteran or a newbie, mindfulness has something to offer runners of every ilk. The following steps will help you become more mindful in your everyday runs and workouts. You can refer to Chapter 6 if you're looking for specific tips on racing. Now armed with all the goods to get you started, proceed to *focus-fathom-flow*.

Chapter 3
STEP ONE: FOCUS

"Being present while running connects you to your body, mind and surroundings. I find deep inspiration from nature and often feel wonderfully overwhelmed with the sheer beauty of it all. When I step out the door, it's so much more than a run."

BASED ON WHERE runner and photographer Sarah Attar lives, these sentiments she shared with me may come as no surprise. The area around her home in Mammoth Lakes, California, 30 miles to the east of Yosemite National Park in the Eastern Sierra Nevada Mountains, is characterized as "geologically active" with hot springs and rhyolite domes. Back 760,000 years ago, a massive volcanic eruption spewed hot ash over the region and evacuated a colossal magma chamber of liquid rock from beneath the surface of the Earth. Fiery hot gas reaching temperatures upward of 1,830°F (1,000°C) and a storm of fragmented volcanic matter sped across the landscape at hundreds of miles per hour, transforming it into what it is today. Cradled in a stunning valley surrounded by calm alpine meadows, scenic canyons lined by ancient woodlands, and serene mountain lakes, it's one of the more naturally majestic places on Earth.

So perhaps it has something to do with the matchless splendor of her environs, but as a photographer, Attar's eye for beauty is undeniable. With a unique penchant to tune in to a kaleidoscope of sensory input through her practice of mindfulness, she garners inspiration as she both shoots and runs the trails. It turns out that this contributes to her success in both fields. Indeed, she was the first female runner to represent Saudi Arabia at the Olympics, running the 800 meters on the track at the 2012 London Games. She again made history running the marathon at the 2016 Games in Rio de Janeiro. She told me:

> *"My personal rhythm and breath interacts with the rhythm of the land. It's as though the tree-lined trail becomes a line of thoughts and the streams I am passing become my stream of consciousness. I find myself constantly connecting to the views, which really brings a sense of presence to the runs. I watch how the light dances across the mountains, listen to the flap of a bird's wings, observe how the storms move in and out across the landscapes, feel the changing weather across my face, smell the storms and the seasons shifting. It all becomes quite magical."*

She continued to explain how her daily training runs become meditations on texture, color, weather, and motion, saying "I think that the higher level of energy exertion while running has something to do with a heightened awareness and experience of the land we run through." Her runs are about much more than staying in shape or preparing for competition. They center on dropping in to the moment and experiencing both the beauty and the challenges of life.

Dropping In

In alpine skiing, "dropping in" is all about taking new terrain by storm. Symbolically, it's the act of focusing in on the body, mind, and environment and then taking a leap of faith. Whether a skier is dropping into a bowl of powder or hucking off a 300-foot cliff, full commitment is vital. The same goes for the mindful running process. Just as Attar suggests, it is through a willingness to fully immerse yourself in the act of running where the real growth happens.

When you "drop in" to mindful running, you set the stage for increased awareness of your surroundings, physical sensations and thoughts. This step is all about focusing in on the present moment—something you may find you haven't done on a run in a while. In *Running and Being* the great running philosopher George Sheehan wrote: Each day I discover how to breathe ... Each day I search out how to run ...

Keep in mind that learning to run mindfully takes practice. Since some amount of mental drift is normal, I like to let my monkey mind swing from the cognitive treetops all it wants for the first five minutes of a run. The concept of the "monkey mind" comes from ancient Buddhism and is often used to describe the agitated, unsettled nature of human cognition. It provides a rather prescient mental image of the way many of us feel in today's hustle and bustle world. Instead of high-octane engines humming along in peak cognitive condition, our brains often more closely resemble a barrelful of cracked-out, shrieking primates.

Whether it's mulling over the responsibilities of the day or drawing upon the inspiration of movement to write the introduction of a story I'm working on, those first moments of a run give my body and brain time to warm up and get in sync, but it isn't enough time for thoughts to calcify into emotions and moods. It doesn't take long before I'm able to easily drop into my run and establish present-moment awareness.

This step involves introspection and observation. It's not about changing anything or drawing judgments, but just becoming aware of things as they exist in the moment. This requires you to shift from "thinking" mode to "sensing" mode. If you notice your mind has wandered and ramped back up into thinking mode—processing, over-analyzing, and turning over thoughts—gently bring it back to the present. Spend a few minutes on each of the following three scanning exercises—first focusing on the passing surroundings, then your body in motion, and finally your mind—concentrating on one thing at a time. With some practice, the *focus* step may only take a couple minutes in total. Step Two will cover what action, if any, you should take based on your observations.

Tune In: Pay close attention to what you're doing when you lace up your running shoes. Feel the lace in your hand and watch as you tie the knot. Notice how the shoe feels on your foot.

Focus: Environment

Whether I'm traveling for work or pleasure, running shoes are a permanent fixture in my carry-on. From chasing down family history in Berlin, to adventure honeymooning in British Columbia, to studying in Ireland, and reporting in various cities across the U.S., I've always loved experiencing new places on foot. It is perhaps this fact that makes the images of my travels so vivid in my mind. As research suggests, there's something about aerobic exercise that boosts the brain's memory hardware.

No one knows this better than Becky Wade. After applying for and receiving a unique fellowship at the age of 23, she was afforded the chance to travel around the world. This wasn't a typical backpacking excursion, however. Wade set out to explore the impressive range of running cultures that exist, traveling to 22 countries and staying with 72 different host families in the process.

In her book, *Run the World*, she chronicles her adventures through nine of those countries, including driving around London with Usain Bolt, partying at Olympic champion Haile Gebrselassie's house in Ethiopia, and watching *Walker, Texas Ranger* with a group of Kenyan Olympians recovering from the 2012 London Olympic Games.

In total, she ended up logging 3,500 miles (5,632 km): Racing a 5K through a shopping mall in Sweden, running the gingko tree-lined trails of Yoyogi Park in Tokyo, tackling the rugged terrain eucalyptus forests of the Ethiopian countryside, and navigating the rolling hills outside Auckland, New Zealand. While she didn't plan on writing a book about it at the time, she was determined to take it all in and fully experience every step of the trip.

"Running definitely serves as a unique link between people and places," Wade told me. "There's something so intimate about covering ground by foot that it's hard not to form a meaningful connection with the nature, wildlife, scents, and overall environment."

Putting energy into savoring her surroundings and embracing the connections she made with other runners in these places helped reinvigorate her love for the sport. "After five years of NCAA competition, I didn't want to burn myself out," she told me. "Running in these naturally beautiful places with all these amazing people got me more fired up for running than ever before."

Indeed, experiencing new environments on foot imbues it with a special meaning well beyond what you would enjoy from the comfortable seat of a tour bus. Wade told me:

"When I'm fully present and really absorbing my surroundings, running is so exhilarating—I'm not worrying about hitting a certain pace, wondering how competitors are training or wishing I was anywhere else in the world. I've trained thousands of places and every

one of them has had a unique combination of sights,
sounds, and smells that have left an imprint on my mind."

* * *

While we might not all have the chance to be literal globe-trotters like Wade, tuning in to your surroundings no matter where you are serves to amplify the running experience. The more I began to embrace mindful running in my own training, I realized how much I had been missing. My daily miles became increasingly vivid and three-dimensional. I started appreciating the fish puckering the surface of the water as I ran along the lakeshore near my home, the gently falling flakes during the first snowfall in November, and that glorious breeze in early spring. I tuned in to the sound of my dog, Welly, loping along next to me on the trail, frequently glancing up for approval. It turned out that as my mind wandered, I was squandering the chance to take in all sorts of joy-inducing sights, sounds, and smells.

Tune In: As you step out the door to run, take two deep breaths and listen for any sounds in your environment. Do you hear traffic, birds, the wind? Are the sounds prominent or do you have to listen closely to hear them?

This first step of the mindful running practice calls you to engage your five senses. I like to imagine how my young daughter would respond to the things I notice, as she's often rapt by the seemingly ordinary—a dandelion or a bird chirping in a nearby tree make for much enjoyment. That childlike mindset puts my head in the right place. Tune in to each sense one at a time as you do this scan or, as Judson Brewer is fond of saying, "Let your senses rip!" Keep in mind that this is purely about noticing without judgment or expectation.

Environmental Scan

- What do you hear?

  Begin by noticing any sounds. If you're in the city, you may first hear the distant roar of an airplane overhead or the flow of traffic from a nearby highway. On a trail, singing birds or the howling wind might be more prominent. One of my favorite sounds I encounter on runs in Minnesota comes from ice melting on the lakes in the spring. Haunting reverberations straight out of a *Star Wars* battle scene echo across the frozen surface as the ice thaws and shifts. There will also be the sounds of your footsteps and respiration. Remember, don't impose expectations on how your foot strike or breathing should sound, just listen.

- What do you smell?

  Next, shift your attention to your sense of smell. It could be fresh-baked bread from a bakery, like the one in my neighborhood, or even a fast-food joint along your route. Depending on the time of year, certain scents from nature will be more obvious. I always love taking in the smell of blooming lilacs in the spring and the drying leaves in the fall.

- What do you taste?

  Observe any discernible flavors. This is easy if you're fueling with nutritionals or sports drinks, but those aren't the only tastes you'll necessarily come across. For instance, in the winter I've perceived a distinct brininess to the air after city crews spread salt on icy roads. Other times those tastes come from within. That metallic tang you get during an intense workout is thought to be from the red blood cells that accumulate in the lungs during hard efforts.

- What do you feel?

  Bring your focus to your sense of touch next. Perhaps you just wiped sweat from your brow and came away with a gritty residue. Or maybe you stopped at a drinking fountain to splash cold water on your face and tie your shoe. You'll also feel your feet as they make contact with the ground.

- What do you see?

  Take in the scenery. Notice the colors, shapes, and textures of the landscape. Check out the terrain underfoot. Focus on other runners or cyclists on the trail as they pass in the opposite direction. I always make sure to spend a few moments watching Welly trotting a few feet ahead of me, her tail wagging and ears flopping with each bound. It's hard not to appreciate the moment when I watch her run.

Tune In: When you pass someone on the trail, take note of what they look like—their facial features, their hair, what they are wearing. Would you recognize them if you came across them in another setting? Do you find you get so caught up in your thoughts that you often overlook things?

Focus: Body

Elinor Fish came from a competitive running background, but as she got older, she found that her body was unable to handle what it once could. After being diagnosed with psoriatic arthritis in her foot, she knew she couldn't train with wild abandon the way she had in high school and college. What's more, she discovered she was becoming far more susceptible to fatigue. Despite all that, running remained her livelihood, an activity that brought her contentment and calm. Desperate to get back to it, she launched a search for a solution.

"I was at my lowest point, reading about all these different kinds of diets and therapies and naturopaths, alternative treatments, medications and vitamin supplements. I was so overwhelmed," she told me from her home in Carbondale, Colorado. "I just needed one clear thing to follow in order to get me back to living an active lifestyle and not being completely overwhelmed with fatigue and stress all the time."

It was about that time that a potential solution came across her radar: mindfulness. "I've always been a runner and I had long been interested in mindfulness, but it was hard for me to sit and meditate," she said. "So I started making mindful running my practice. Every run the idea was to relax and tune in to myself. It had nothing to do with running fast or far or hard."

With time and practice, she changed the way she viewed training. Instead of being focused on speed or mileage, it became more about health and wellness. She emphasized to me: "What I learned was that we shouldn't be trying to override or ignore our body's signals, but to actually tune in and pay closer attention to

Mindfulness trains you to listen to and learn from your body's cues.

what our bodies are telling us and then use that information to run smarter and to take better care of ourselves."

Having long worked in the running industry, Fish decided that she wanted to share her mindful running revelations with others. She told me:

"As I talked to more and more people about these ideas, it became obvious that many runners needed this. It's really hard to slow down enough and notice what's happening to us, both mentally and physically. I think that runners are particularly good at pushing past those limits without stopping to ask if what you're doing is sustainable."

In 2010, she founded Run Wild Retreats + Wellness, a company that holds mindful running retreats in far-flung locations from Reykjavik to Moab to Costa Brava. Over the years, Fish has met hundreds of runners who are overtrained, stressed, and burned out, all looking for ways to better manage energy and motivation in both running and life. She works to teach them how tuning in and learning to listen to your body with mindful awareness can be a game changer when it comes to health and well-being. Serving as living proof of the power of mindful running, Fish is not only operating a successful small business, she continues to unearth joie de vivre along the trails on which she runs.

***

According to fossil evidence analyzed by researchers from the University of Utah and Harvard, humans started to run around two million years ago. These experts hypothesize that while we are nowhere near as fast as other mammals, like the cheetah or pronghorn antelope, we are natural endurance athletes. Our long legs, springy tendons, arched feet, and strong glute muscles are all thought to have adapted to help us evolve as runners and succeed as a species.

For being born to run, we modern-day human beings sure seem to get hurt a lot. While the numbers vary, most statistics suggest that anywhere from 37 percent to upward of 79 percent of runners encounter an injury during any given year. The biggest culprit? Training errors. As Fish explained to me, you'd be surprised how out of touch we are with our own bodies—how often we push when we should back off, either out of bullheadedness or inexperience. Building mileage too abruptly, neglecting rest and recovery, and running too many high-intensity workouts are at the top of the list of training blunders runners make.

"I often see runners who become so outcome-focused that they start a training plan and don't pay attention to how their body is responding to that training," Fish said. "It's all too easy to show up to the starting line of a race injured, exhausted, and feeling far from your best when you aren't listening to your body."

Tune In: Before you start your run, stand for a moment and see if you can sense the gravitational pull of the Earth on your body.

Tuning into how your body feels on a run cues you in to when you should push forward and when you should back off.

The way you run—your running form—can also lead to injuries. With that said, it is important to bear in mind that while every runner follows a set of predictable phases through the gait cycle, the particular way individual runners execute each phase is wholly unique. The runners I coach often ask me for pointers on running technique and I always emphasize to them that there is no single correct way to run. No matter what popular fitness media tells you about proper foot strike, body positioning or stride frequency, the fact remains: There's no one right way to run.

When I was reporting on a story for the now-defunct *Running Times* magazine a number of years ago, I spoke with Harvard's Daniel Lieberman about this topic. I was immediately engrossed by the evolutionary biology professor's whip-smart wit and intense curiosity for how the body moves. His 2009 study, published in *Nature*, gained fame for its revelation that Kenyan runners who ran barefoot tended to be forefoot strikers and hit the ground with less impact. That, along with Christopher McDougall's international bestseller, *Born to Run*, inspired a maelstrom of discussions regarding the "best" way to run. The conversation mainly focused on which part of the foot we should strike the ground with (forefoot, midfoot, or heel) and what type of footwear would help support that strike pattern.

While this prompted important debate about running gait mechanics, Lieberman was clearly frustrated with the over-simplification of his work and the media frenzy to produce sensational headlines. He told me, "My research and what people have said about my research are two different things. Adopting a 'this is good' and 'this is bad' approach isn't helping anybody."

For the same story, Stephen Pribut, widely recognized for his expertise in podiatric sports medicine and biomechanics, echoed this point to me: "I don't think there is any good reason to be dogmatic about it and say something is good for everyone or bad for everyone. It's whatever works for you." When it comes to human biology, variation is the norm. Every runner is an experiment of one.

Case in point: In 2010, two of evolutionary biology professor Peter Larson's undergraduate students from Saint Anselm College in New Hampshire made the trek to Boston on Marathon Monday. They filmed the first 1,000 runners that passed the 17.5-mile point of the race in Newton, Massachusetts, setting the camera at 300 frames per second to get a detailed look at elite running mechanics. If you watch the video, you'll see the eventual winner, Robert Kiprono Cheruiyot of Kenya, lope by, as well as other top finishers like Ethiopians Tekeste Kebede and Deriba Merga and Americans Ryan Hall and Meb Keflezighi.

As they gracefully float from right to left across the frame in slow motion, you see that Cheruiyot runs upright, ever so slightly landing on his heels with his arms flexed and high. Hall, alternatively, lands midfoot, subtly leaning forward and carrying his arms closer to his waist. Keflezighi is a clear heel striker, holding his arms higher and running more upright like Cheruiyot. The takeaway from this footage is that even the best of the best don't fit into any particular ideal mold in terms of running form. It's likely that we run the way we run because it's what works best for our individual physiology.

When researchers have looked into the relationship between running gait and injuries, results have been mixed. For instance, heel striking—what 94 percent of runners do, according to one 2013 study published in the *International Journal of Sports Physiology and Performance*—has been shown to be hard on your knees, but running on your toes places greater strain on your Achilles. The late nine-time New York City Marathon champion and Olympian Grete Waitz wrote in her book *Run Your First Marathon*: "Contrary to a common myth, while there are general guidelines, there is no exact 'right' way to run … I am amazed by the many ways people move forward." If you're experiencing injuries or logging lackluster performances, then it might be time to consult an expert. Otherwise, meddling with your gait may end up doing more harm than good.

Tune In: Next time you get up, pay attention to your body as you walk. What is your posture like? Do you swing your arms much? What does the ground feel like underfoot with each step?

A few years ago, I visited the biomechanics lab for the running brand Brooks, which is just outside Seattle, Washington. It was there that I got a first-hand view of how running-shoe companies use cutting-edge technology to get an objective view of how runners run. I watched as the lab technician outfitted one of their sponsored runners with cylindrical biomotion sensors on key areas of her body. As she began running on the treadmill, her likeness sprang to life on the big screen in front of us, represented by a series of

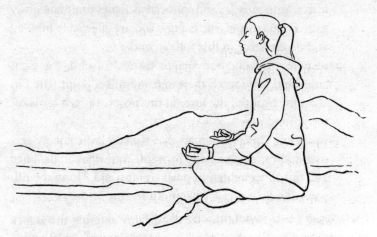

Applying a meditative mindset to your running aids you in developing an objective view of training.

moving vectors. With the bright green lines operating in tandem, I saw the gait cycle through a more mechanical lens for the first time.

In understanding the biomechanics at play as you observe your body running through space, you'll gain a greater appreciation for the way your body moves, as well as become more attuned to the times when something is going awry. I almost always perceive tension in my shoulders and my jaw and I instantly relax simply by noticing it. Don't get hung up on how your stride appears to onlookers or whether you're running with "proper" form. Remain objective, as if you're watching yourself as a body of moving vectors on a screen.

The Running Gait Cycle

- Stance Phase: This phase involves three distinct steps.

    Initial contact At the beginning of stance phase, the right foot first hits the ground and pronates (rolls inward). Your right knee and ankle flex as you land, absorbing impact forces. Your muscles and connective tissues simultaneously gather and store elastic energy. You are effectively braking and decelerating in this split second.

    Midstance As your bodyweight carries forward, the right ankle and knee reach their maximum flex point. The hip takes the brunt of the force at this point. The left leg is off the ground now.

    Propulsion This is when all that stored elastic energy gets used to propel your body forward. Your right ankle, knee and hip all straighten to push you forward. Upon toe-off, you enter float phase when both feet are in the air.

- Swing Phase: While the left leg begins entering the stance phase, the right leg starts to swing forward. This occurs when you lift your right heel up toward your backside. Like a slingshot, the extension of your hip pulls back and fires forward, leading with the knee. The lower part of the right leg then passes under your body and prepares for contact with the ground once again.

- Upper Body: All the while, your upper body is working in tandem with the lower body and your left arm comes forward as your right leg drives forward. While your lower body is braking, the upper body creates a propulsive force and when your legs hit the propulsion phase, your upper body creates a braking force. This is how forward momentum is achieved.

Kinesthetic Awareness and Proprioception

As you begin to pay attention to your body as you run, you may come to wonder how exactly your brain knows when to signal your feet to strike the ground. The answer has to do with proprioception and kinesthetic awareness—further proof that we humans really are born to run. Kinesthetic awareness is the body's sense of where it is in space—think of the precise body sense a gymnast must have to do a back flip on a balance beam. While running might seem less technical, when you break down the gait cycle, you realize that it is a series of single-leg balancing poses. Proprioception is the body's sense of how the joints, muscles, and fascia all work together to produce coordinated movement.

Not sure how good your proprioception is? Try this: Stand on one leg with your eyes closed. If you find yourself wobbling, your proprioception may be lacking. There are a number of potential culprits. Most commonly, past injuries, like ankle sprains, are detrimental to proprioception. The following is a series of simple balance exercises that can help you improve your proprioception. To enhance the difficulty of any of these, close your eyes.

Balancing Act

Single-Leg Balancing Balance on one foot for one minute with your hands on your hips, then switch sides.

Single-Leg Hops With your hands on your hips again, stand on one foot and take one hop forward, pause, and then take one hop backward. Complete ten forward and backward hops.

Single-Leg Squats With your hands on your hips and all of your weight on one leg, maintain balance while performing ten single leg squats on each side. Be sure to keep your knee in line with your ankle as you squat.

Breathing and Rhythm

You'll often hear mindfulness experts espouse the importance of getting "curious" about your breath. "What could possibly be interesting about my respiration?" you may wonder. When you really think about it, plenty. Consider this amazing process: As we run, we exhale carbon dioxide molecules from our bodies and we inhale oxygen molecules from the air. If this process ceases for even a few moments, the brain suffers permanent damage. Anywhere from 18,000 to 20,000 liters of air pass through the nose on a daily basis, filtering with 100 percent efficiency and humidifying the air we breathe to prevent the lining of the lungs and bronchial tubes from getting dry. A recent study by anthropology and genetics researchers at Pennsylvania State University even suggests that nostril shape was dictated by ancestral climate—that people whose ancestors come from colder and dryer regions tend to have narrow nostrils in order to more efficiently warm and humidify the air as it enters the nose.

Tune In: With all this in mind, close your eyes for a moment and take five deep breaths. Follow each breath to its end. Examine how each one is slightly different from the last as you focus on the air going in and out of your nostrils and your chest and belly rising and falling.

This intricate process also involves your heart. After breathing oxygen-rich air into your lungs, the oxygen is moved into the blood via capillaries within your lungs. The heart is then in charge of transferring the oxygen-rich blood from the lungs to the rest of the body. Simultaneously, carbon dioxide is transported back to the lungs and you expel it as waste via your outbreath.

If you're not impressed yet, consider this: We naturally sync up our breathing with our body as we run. Exercise physiologists have a fancy term for this: Entrainment of locomotion and ventilation. Dogs, horses, lizards, jackrabbits and of course, humans have all been shown to synchronize the rhythm of breath and stride. You might strike a 3:3 rhythm on an easy jog, for instance, which would involve stepping left-right-left as you breathe in and right-left-right as you breathe out. As you pick up the pace, that rhythm quickens, so you might be doing 2:2, left-right while you breathe in and left-right while you breathe out, or even 1:1 if you're really pushing it in a workout. Famed running coach Jack Daniels favors a 2:2 rhythm for breathing efficiency, while other studies have found runners are successful anywhere between 2:1 and 4:1.

Similar to running gait, if what you're doing is working, I wouldn't worry about tinkering with your natural rhythm. With that said, while there isn't unified agreement on which particular pattern is best, research suggests that adopting some sort of rhythm is important. A 2013 study published in *PLOS ONE* that studied the breathing dynamics of runners on treadmills concluded that a rhythmic breathing pattern lightens the work of the respiratory muscles while you run, which translates into reduced fatigue and possibly improved performance.

When you inhale, pay attention to how you take air in. Best-case scenario, you take deep breaths into your belly, not shallow breaths into your chest. While there are many benefits to nasal breathing when you're at rest, hard running necessitates breathing from your mouth too in order to get enough oxygen to your working muscles. The bottom line is you should do whatever works for you. If you're interested in the potential calming effect of breath prior to a race or other anxiety-inducing event, we'll cover that in Chapter 6.

All of this information can serve to pique your curiosity as you tune in to your body while you're running. Remember this isn't about judging or changing anything, just noticing. If your mind wanders, gently bring it back to wherever you left off in the scan.

Body Scan

- Start at the top of your head. Bring your awareness to your scalp, forehead, eyes, and face. Are you holding any tension in your jaw or furrowing your brow? See if you can let it soften.

- Move down to your neck and shoulders. Are you tight, relaxed, or somewhere in between?

- Take note of your breath and the air filling your lungs. Are you inhaling and exhaling through both your nose and mouth? Is the air warm or cold?

- How do your arms, hands, and fingers feel? What is your arm carriage like? Are you using your arms to power forward?

- Next, scan down your spine. How is your posture? Are you hunching forward or slightly arching your back?

- Move on to your core, including your lower back, abdominals, and hips. Do you feel your hips rotating excessively or mostly driving forward? Are your abs engaged as you stride?

- Travel down your legs, taking stock of your quads, hamstrings, knees, shins, and calves. Are there any twinges of pain or discomfort? Do your legs feel fresh or tired?

- Finally, finish by observing your feet. Are you striking the ground with your heel, midfoot, or forefoot? Can you feel them roll inward as you make contact with the ground?

Focus: Mind

While it's difficult to pin down an exact number, it's safe to say that we each have tens of thousands of cognitions on any given day. When our minds are left unchecked, those thoughts buzz around frantically like bees in a jar, wildly battering about our brains. The result is often negative rumination and intrusive thinking, which cues the fight-or-flight response.

Indeed, it seems this phenomenon is truly universal. When a group of researchers from around the world came together to interview university students at 15 sites in 13 countries across 6 continents, 94 percent reported having unwanted or intrusive thoughts on a regular basis. Whether it's about a bad workout that you can't let go of, a recent disagreement you had with a friend, or worries about the health of a family member, it's easy to slip into this cyclical mindset and slide down the rabbit hole of anger and angst without even realizing it. Stress hormones begin to surge through the body, heart rate spikes, breathing gets shallow, and decision-making skills suffer.

Daniel Goleman, a psychologist and author of the *New York Times* bestseller *Emotional Intelligence: Why It Can Matter More Than IQ*, refers to this cognitive loss of control as "amygdala hijack." The amygdala is an almond-sized chunk of gray matter in the cerebral hemisphere that houses our emotional responses to things. When the amygdala fires up, a cascade of emotions pulse through the body. Fortunately, mindfulness has the power to increase your ability to recruit higher order thinking in these situations, while ratcheting down the fight-or-flight reaction, thus quelling stress and anxiety. It trains your mind to observe thoughts and emotions, rather than automatically engage with them. As mindfulness experts often say, it creates "space" so you can calmly decide how to respond.

The "glitter jar," or what I like to call the "Jitter Jar," is one activity mindfulness teachers use with children and teenagers to help illustrate this point, but it can also come in handy when you're trying to calm pre-race jitters. To make one, simply fill a clear jar or bottle ¾ full with water and a bit of glitter glue. Then drop in 3–5 teaspoons of glitter (for step-by-step instructions, check out the "Mindful Hacks" in Chapter 8). The glitter represents feelings, thoughts, and emotions.

Seal up the jar. Now, think about your day and give the Jitter Jar a shake for something that made you angry—maybe you got chewed out by your boss or you slammed your finger in your car door this morning. You can also shake it for something more positive—perhaps you got a promotion at work or you won the lottery. All of these things can make you feel jittery and amped up in an unproductive way.

By this point the glitter will be swirling, making it impossible to see through the jar. This symbolizes when your brain gets flooded with cortisol and adrenaline in response to the various stresses and excitement you encounter in your day. When that happens, your prefrontal cortex goes offline and you can't think clearly because all these feelings, thoughts, and emotions—the glitter—are swirling around, clouding your judgment. In order to see, you must simply watch and wait patiently for the glitter to settle at the bottom of the jar. Once the water has calmed, you are in a better position to call up the necessary wisdom to make sound decisions.

Those thoughts and emotions disturbing the glassy calmness of the mind are often tied up in anxieties, stresses, and responsibilities of the past and future. Mindfulness teaches us not to block those thoughts—as human beings, they are impossible to avoid—but also not to get attached or react to them impulsively. As you do this mental scan, you are simply tuning in to your brain's mental chatter—waiting for the glitter to come to rest—which can help you discern when it's important to allow the mind to settle.

Tune In: Take note of the thoughts and emotions that are going through your mind at this very moment. Are they positive, negative or neutral? Productive or unproductive? How are these thoughts coloring your mood? Are you having any sort of physical response to the thoughts or emotions?

Mindfulness calls you to notice thoughts and emotions and let them float through your mind like passing clouds in the sky, rather than getting hung up on wrestling them into submission or attempting to deny them altogether. We can't change the weather, so why waste energy compounding the storm?

Understand that turning your attention to your mind to take stock of the content of your cognitions is no easy feat. Even master meditators are susceptible to having their minds wander from the task at hand. And that is precisely the point. Each time you notice that you are distracted, gently bring your attention back to the present, again and again. This practice is akin to running intervals on the track or pumping iron at the gym. Repeatedly redirecting your attention fortifies neural pathways and strengthens the muscle of the mind.

Mind Scan

- Start by noticing and acknowledging the top three thoughts running through your mind.

- Take stock of the speed of your thoughts. Is your mind racing, are you feeling more lethargic, or are you somewhere in between?

- Identify whether you're attaching emotions to the thoughts. Are you worrying about work or stressing about what you have to do after the run?

- What is the storyline you're following? Are the thoughts you're having being fed by a certain identity you've created for yourself?

- Notice whether stress in your everyday life is shaping your attitude toward your run. Are the anxieties stemming from other venues causing you to feel bored, hurried, tired, or uncomfortable?

- Remember, being mindful is all about noticing the thoughts without judgment. Identify each thought as it pops into your head and let it move along without obsessing over it, trying to push it away, or clinging to it.

Hopefully, by observing your surroundings, physical sensations, thoughts, and emotions on the run, you've tapped into a wellspring of information. In the next chapter, you'll learn what to do with the raw data of experience that you gathered in Step One. While mindfulness calls for acceptance of things as they are in the present moment, that doesn't mean you can't take action to alter the trajectory of your path. Read on to find out when and how to best approach this aspect of your mindful running practice.

CHAPTER 4
STEP TWO: FATHOM

"I'm very process oriented. When I'm tired or negative thoughts are creeping into my head, I work on not only being aware of those things, but also figuring out a way to address them. In stepping back, taking a look at the big picture, and understanding processes and results, I'm constantly learning about myself as an athlete and a person."

WHEN PROFESSIONAL TRIATHLETE Sarah Piampiano told me this, she credited endurance sports with helping her hone this method of first bringing awareness to and then devising strategies for change. This wasn't always something she did so adeptly, however. Learning how to tune in and take necessary action is the mechanism by which a major transformation in her life was put into motion.

Back in 2009, 28-year-old Piampiano was the vision of a high-achieving college graduate working to prove herself in the competitive world of finance in New York City. She worked hectic 100-hour weeks as a Wall Street investment banker and traveled for her job 14 days out of every month to far-flung locales in Asia, South and Central America and Europe. She furiously puffed through two packs of cigarettes a day, spent evenings throwing back cocktails at Upper West Side bars and restaurants, and never seemed to be able to find time to exercise. The candle was most certainly burning at both ends.

Then came an evening out with an old college buddy. As beverages were consumed and the clock ticked into the early hours of the morning, the idea of racing a triathlon spontaneously arose. Soon there was a bet on the table as to who would be faster. That's all it took for the competitive Piampiano to sign on the dotted line of the race registration form for the fast-approaching Mooseman Triathlon in central New Hampshire. This was despite the fact that she wasn't the least bit prepared, nor was she even sure what exactly a triathlon entailed. All she knew was that she didn't feel great the way things were going and she wanted to turn toward a healthier path. Plus, she wasn't one to ever back down from a friendly wager.

Early one Saturday morning in June, "Little Red," as she is often referred to on account of her strawberry blonde locks, made her way to the beach at Newfound Lake in Wellington State Park located in Bristol. Of the three sports, she anticipated that the swim would be the hardest, but her confidence was bolstered as she charged into the pristine 4,000-acre lake that is said to be one of the cleanest in the world.

Following the 1,500-meter swim came a 27-mile bike ride past classic New England farmhouses and village greens. Whether it was the speed she was sailing on her bike or the refreshing morning swim prior, Piampiano felt inimitably inspired. "This is something I could actually be good at, really good," she thought.

By the time she came into transition for the run, which she knew would be her strongest leg, she had already decided this wasn't going to be a one-and-done, bucket list type of endeavor. Racing 10 kilometers along the shores of Newfound Lake and coming into the finish ahead of her college friend and bettor, the light bulb was fully on. On her website, Piampiano wrote, "Not only did I win the bet, I loved every moment of the experience and walked away with a fire in my belly."

That single race experience prompted a sharp U-turn in her path, shifting her perspective and allowing her to step back and take a wider view of the life she was living versus the life she could have. She told me:

> *"Before I started training and doing triathlons I was very aware of how awful I felt, but I also lacked the motivation to do something about it. After that first triathlon, I started exercising more, eating better, and I stopped smoking—for me it was extremely motivating because I was coming from a place of total lack of health. I could breathe better, I had more energy, and I was more productive at work."*

It didn't take long for her to discover that she had a rare proclivity for the endurance disciplines. After quickly rising to the top of the age-group ranks, she quit her job and later moved from the Big Apple to Santa Monica, California to train. With just a couple years of experience, she started racing professionally and in 2012 won one of her first races at the Ironman 70.3 New Orleans. She is now among the top women on the professional circuit vying for the title of Ironman World Champion in Kona, Hawaii.

Not surprisingly, she says that tuning in and learning to listen and respond to what her body and mind are telling her has been essential to her success. "I've become more aware of what my body's needs are," she told me. "It's been a huge learning curve figuring out how to read the signs and knowing when to pull back and when to press forward."

Focusing in and becoming aware of your body and mind is an important first step in your mindful running practice, but the action you take based on those observations is equally, if not more, powerful. In Piampiano's case, she got a taste of how it felt to be an athlete. The stark contrast from her life as a two-pack-a-day, overworked Wall Street executive couldn't be ignored. Once she tuned in, she charted a course to make adjustments.

Stories like Piampiano's remain among my favorite to report on because they are so relatable. Piampiano and athletes like her inspire us regular Joes and Janes to push ourselves to wake up, make big changes, and be better than we thought possible.

Gathering Beta

As Piampiano's story demonstrates, becoming aware of how things are in the present is the first step toward improvement. But simply noticing, for instance, that smoking two packs of cigarettes a day makes you feel bad, isn't enough. When you tune in to those feelings and truly realize the consequences of your actions and the machinations of your mind, it is important to make plans to respond. The step of fathoming allows you to meditate on the data you gathered in Step One and decide if adjustments are necessary.

Rock climbers call this "gathering beta." "Beta" is information about a particular route, including the climb's level of difficulty, the quality of the rock, the positioning of hand and foot holds, and where to hook your foot around the edge of an arête or jump from one hold to another. Altogether, this information offers a path upward. Experienced climbers take in beta to get the big picture, but as they climb, they often imagine a small halo surrounding their body, tackling what's directly in front of them. This not only conserves energy, it also allows the climber to make reasoned decisions.

Instead of trying to muscle up the crag in one go, embrace the climbing ethos as you mindfully fathom the things you noticed in Step One. While focusing on the present moment and fathoming observations can feel difficult at first, with practice, new neural pathways are forged. In the same way that running a certain pace feels easier as you log more miles, brain-training strengthens that mental muscle.

Through interviews, research, and almost 25 years of my own running, I have identified a number of common themes that can come up on the run. While this is by no means an exhaustive list, it will help offer you ideas on how to respond to some of the thoughts, feelings, sensations, and emotions you're likely to encounter. Suffering, fatigue, boredom, anxiety, and self-judgment are chief among those. On the flipside, you may also find your mind in a loop of more pleasant thoughts or in brainstorming mode, detaching you from what's happening in the moment. In some cases, simply observing and labeling the thought or physical sensation (see page 83) will neutralize it and almost instantly enhance your running experience. In other situations, it might require more deliberate and immediate action.

Suffering: What Doesn't Kill Us

I first met Dean Karnazes in 2013 at a press junket for The North Face Endurance Challenge Championship, a premiere 50-mile event on the ultrarunning circuit, which also includes several shorter races. A group of journalists and The North Face-sponsored athletes gathered in the Holiday Inn lobby in Mill Valley in preparation for a morning run. Stars from the ultra scene like Rob Krar and Rory Bosio were there, the latter of which I had just interviewed for an espnW story on the heels of her big win at the 103-mile (166 km) Ultra-Trail du Mont-Blanc in the Alps, widely considered to be one of the hardest ultras in the world.

Karnazes was nearly twice the age of the other elites in the group, but you wouldn't know it by looking at him. Dubbed the "ultramarathon man," back in 2006 he ran a marathon in all 50 states in just 50 days. He's won the infamous 135-mile Badwater Ultramarathon in Death Valley in 120°F (49°C) heat, run 350 miles (563 km) in under 81 hours with no sleep, and completed a marathon in the South Pole in temperatures that dipped to

A mindful approach to running can help reveal greater joy in the simple act of putting one foot in front of the other.

-13°F (-25°C). He's even been named one of the top 100 most influential people in the world by *Time* magazine.

That morning in Mill Valley, we ran along the shores of the pristine estuary of Richardson Bay, which gently flows into the Pacific Ocean. Karnazes casually chatted about the upcoming race that would be held in the Marin Headlands—his home stomping grounds. He spoke of the stunning vistas and gnarly climbs we would encounter on the trails the next day. As with most press events I attend, I wasn't there just as a journalist, but also as a runner.

Later that evening we all went to a dinner at the Karnazes' compound in Marin County. In addition to his impressive living quarters, he embodies a unique quality that immediately makes him easy to pick out of a crowd. Whether it's his physique, built from running countless miles year after year, or his calm intensity, even if you don't know his story, it's clear he's no mere mortal.

Karnazes wrote in his book *Ultramarathon Man: Confessions of an All-Night Runner,* "there's magic in misery"—ethos he would have to embrace to tackle his particular brand of endurance exploits. During a recent conversation, he let me in on his secret for handling suffering on the run: mindfulness. He explained to me:

> *"About ten years ago I started using this approach to deal with low points during races—those really difficult times when you just feel like you can't go on. I've tried using positive mantras and other things, but with pain, you can't fake yourself out. Really tuning in to the pain and embracing the struggle is more effective because it dissipates its impact."*

He went on to wax philosophical about the ephemeral and mysterious nature of pain, something he's had plenty of time to think about over many thousands of miles on his feet. "Pain is in the neurons of the beholder," he added, saying that we all perceive it in different ways. For reasons he can't quite explain, meditating on the pain somehow seems to mitigate its power.

* * *

There's no way to get around the fact that running involves a certain amount of suffering. Strength and endurance are built over time, when you strategically subject your body to physiological stress followed by periods of rest. The question is, how do you know when you should embrace suffering and discomfort and when you should throw in the towel because you're inflicting real damage?

Being able to disentangle "good" pain from "bad" pain is no easy feat. Even top professionals are susceptible to misreading the signals, pushing when they should back off and hurtling into a downward spiral of injury and illness. Others hang it up at the first sign of discomfort, which prevents them from ever taking their training to the next level.

Ultrarunner and mindfulness researcher Rick Hecht explained it to me this way: "Mindfulness can help you discriminate the difference between the discomfort associated with a hard effort in training or racing and one that is going to lead to injury. From my personal experience, it helps me pay attention to my body's cues and signals when I'm running."

As you fathom feelings of pain, you learn to decide what action, if any, needs to be taken. When you observe an ache in your calf or a throbbing in your hamstring, stay with it for a few moments and explore the sensations. Ask yourself the following questions:

- Have I felt this pain before?
- Could this be related to an injury?
- Is it sharp, throbbing, or dull?
- Is it a shooting pain or is it more localized?

Answering these queries can shift the discomfort from a physical and emotional experience to a more intellectual one. By examining the sensations with intense curiosity, you're able to objectively devise a plan for your next step. If the beta you've gathered is hinting that you might be headed for an injury, it's important to abandon your run and seek out the advice of a medical expert. A day or two on the bench is always better than a season lost to a serious injury.

If you suspect the discomfort is of the "good" variety—part of the innate discomfort that goes along with exercise—the tenets of mindful running call you to notice it and accept its existence. Examining these feelings with a mind of curiosity helps reveal the ever-changing nature of pain. Many runners believe that distracting their mind and ignoring suffering is the best way through these moments, but as was mentioned in Chapter 1, the research shows that the more you resist a feeling, thought, or emotion, ironically, the more you end up caught in it (The White Bear problem).

For runners, denial of suffering takes a whole lot of mental energy and only serves to heap on an additional layer of angst when you're already uncomfortable. In his book *Full Catastrophe Living,* Jon Kabat-Zinn writes about how the intensity of pain is often a function of the particular lens through which we view it and the ways in which we react to it, rather than the actual physical sensations. Mindful running teaches you to avoid burning energy resisting suffering and to find meaning in embracing it. It trains you to be open to all experiences, sensations, and emotions, even the hard ones.

Fortunately, the archives of exercise science research demonstrate that the memories of suffering and discomfort subside as more time passes after an event. That's why you end up signing up for subsequent races after you've sworn up and down at the finish line of a particularly excruciating event that you'll never run again. While this is still a new field of study, research involving ultrarunners suggests that expecting and accepting some level of suffering— in effect, learning to embrace agony—helps runners deal with pain in a constructive manner.

"In the past, we often talked about ignoring or pushing away discomfort, but mindfulness actually calls you to pay attention to it and notice it in a careful nonjudgmental way," Hecht told me, in reference to the emerging medical literature on pain. "Often someone realizes that it isn't as bad when you're not trying to push it away—that they were ruminating or catastrophizing and making the pain worse. You can actually work with the pain in a different way when you're applying mindfulness instead of getting freaked out."

When I spoke with Hecht, he recounted a particularly dramatic moment during his first attempt running the Western States 100. Around the halfway point, he was struggling to ascend one of the most difficult climbs on the course to Michigan Bluff, a tiny hamlet in the Sierra Nevada Mountains that was once a booming outpost during the gold rush of the 1860s and 1870s. As he made his way toward the sounds of cheering fans that take over the sleepy old mining town once a year, his body began to revolt. His legs ached, exhausted from navigating the rugged terrain. Then came nausea and uncontrollable retching. "I felt terrible and I thought, 'oh my gosh, I'm never going to be able to go on,'" he recalled. "Being able to work with those feelings was still tough, but mindfulness gave me that sense that I could think my way through them."

A whole host of research reveals that pain is not only a physiological construct, but also a psychological one. "Perception of pain" is how it's often referred to in the literature. Mindfulness meditation has been shown to reduce pain and researchers have demonstrated that therapeutic techniques rooted in the principles of mindfulness can train you to more readily accept the inherent discomfort that accompanies exercise. In one study, supported by the National Institutes of Health and published in the *Journal of Neuroscience*, just four sessions of 20 minutes a day of mindfulness training reduced pain intensity ratings in participants who were subjected to a heat probe on their skin by a whopping 40 percent. That's pretty amazing considering the fact that morphine and other pain medications decrease pain intensity by around 25 percent and are accompanied by a long list of side effects like constipation, nausea, and drowsiness.

Exercise 4.1: Next time you feel an itch, instead of scratching it, try focusing in on it. Does it radiate outward or is it more localized? Is it an intense itch or a mild vibration on the skin? Try to avoid reacting to it, just stay with it. In many cases, the itch goes away in the same way that pain seems to lose its power when you bring objective awareness to it.

"We haven't seen any other techniques to address pain that use the same mechanics that mindfulness does," Zeidan of Wake Forest School of Medicine told me. He has devoted his career to studying the neural mechanisms involved in mindfulness meditation and the effect it has on a wide spectrum of chronic pain outcomes. Also a runner, he's developed a rare perspective on how mindfulness might influence perception of pain. "We've been really surprised to see this super ancient technique that is using novel pathways. We are potentially on the verge of discovering a non-opiate pain-relieving pathway in the brain."

When you tune into the moment, you often discover that your mind is intensifying physical discomfort.

Mindfulness serves to disarm suffering—whether it is caused by gnarly terrain, abysmal weather, physical exertion, or negative thinking—by putting space between the feelings of pain and your perception of it. Indeed, researchers at the University of California, Los Angeles demonstrated that simply labeling an emotion and putting it into words significantly reduces its intensity and even prompts a neurological response, as seen on fMRI brain scans. Referred to as "affect labeling," you can diminish the power of uncomfortable feelings and sensations on a run just by mindfully noticing and naming them in your head (see Action Items on page 84). Other research backs that up, showing that the better you are at describing your emotions, the more grounded and secure you will be when encountering stressful and challenging situations.

What's more, when you're mindful of feelings and physical sensations, you can decide when it's best to deploy other psychological skills. In the case of pain, a positive mantra can come in handy. A mantra is a word or phrase that is helpful to repeat in the toughest moments of a run or race. Alexi Pappas' "stay" is a good example. Similarly, I often use "maintain" to encourage me to take one step at a time and sustain my pace until suffering subsides.

Exercise 4.2: Find Your Mantra: Come up with a word or phrase that will motivate and inspire you in times of discomfort and suffering. Prior to a race or run, write it on your hand so it's right there when you need it.

Action Items

- Label the physical sensations and emotions without focusing on whether they are good or bad. Your inner dialogue might look something like this: "Tension", "Burning", "Soreness".
- If you suspect the pain is a result of an impending injury, stop running and consult your physician.
- If the suffering is related to the inherent discomfort associated with exercise, stay with it for a moment.
- As you put some distance between the feeling and the thought, try to zoom out to get a big picture view. As Karnazes wrote in his book *Ultramarathon Man*, sometimes "we confuse comfort with happiness."
- Let go of the discomfort and shift your mind to a different object of your attention in the present moment—the sound of your feet striking the ground or the sunshine sluicing through the canopy of trees overhead.
- If you notice you're having trouble shifting out of suffering mode, invoke a predetermined mantra to repeat in your head until you're through those tough moments.

Fatigue: Mind Over Matter

"Hill, you're a bitch ... it's long and hot-God damn it ... mother eff-er." "Oh my God, I'm so tired. My stomach hurts so bad ...

I'm going to throw up right now." These are the actual recorded thoughts of runners as they ran, gathered by researchers for a study published in the *International Journal of Sport and Exercise Psychology*.

Be honest. While you might not curse into a portable recorder like the runners in the study did, you can relate, right? Runners are often dogged by feelings of exhaustion when they aren't in the right headspace. This turns even an everyday run into a sufferfest. If the observations you made in Step One involved feeling worn down and weary, you should first identify whether it is productive fatigue or lethargy that is related to overtraining or under-fueling. Similar to pain and discomfort, you must disentangle the "good" from the "bad."

The latter type of fatigue occurs when your body and brain are maxed out. It is the result of too many high-intensity workouts, too many miles, a poor fueling strategy, not enough rest and recovery, or stressors in other areas of life that are hampering your running performance. Regardless of the cause, the symptoms related to overtraining syndrome include everything from a general lack of

Bringing mindful awareness to feelings of fatigue can help you determine the best path forward.

energy to unexplained aches, insomnia, moodiness, and changes in appetite.

Fathoming feelings of fatigue can help you identify whether you're on the verge of overtraining. If you answer "yes" to even just a couple of these questions, it may indicate you need to take a break:

- Have you experienced an inexplicable drop in performance or inability to hit your normal training paces?
- Do you spend much of the day feeling drained and lacking energy?
- Is your appetite less than usual?
- Are you feeling more irritable or anxious lately?
- Are your muscles constantly sore and achy?
- Have you been ill more often than usual?
- Have you encountered a string of injuries?

Being mindful of how your body is responding to training is essential. To avoid reaching the point of diminishing returns, many runners subscribe to the 80/20 rule, devoting 80 percent of their mileage to easy running and just 20 percent to higher intensity "quality" workouts. When researchers at the Exercise Physiology Laboratory at the European University of Madrid put this approach to the test, they discovered that over five months of training 50–55 miles (80–88 km) per week, a group of runners who did 80 percent of their miles at an easy pace improved significantly more in a 6.5-mile time trial than those who only did 65 percent at an easy pace. In addition, many coaches suggest increasing mileage from one week to the next by no more than 10 percent. So if you run 20 miles (32 km) one week, you shouldn't bump that up to more than around 22 miles (35 km) the subsequent week, 24 (38 km) the week after that and so forth.

In 2015 I was writing a series of journal entries for Ironman's website about my training for Ironman Wisconsin and I sought out the advice of professional triathlete Linsey Corbin on this very subject. She helped me resist that paradoxical magnetism of overtraining for the 140.6-mile event, firmly insisting that more is not necessarily better. "Take time to rest and don't feel bad about it," she advised. "By taking that time to focus on other things in life, you'll achieve a better training/life balance, which will keep both you and your family and friends happier in the long run."

I figured if a multiple Ironman champion was imploring me to take a little R&R, who was I to argue? As most coaches recommend, I've found that reducing my mileage and intensity in workouts every 3–4 weeks is all I need to keep the wheels from coming off. Remember, rest is part of training.

The other easily addressed factor that can cause fatigue is under-fueling. You've "hit the wall" when you are dizzy with exhaustion and feel unable to take another step. This is the point at which your body has burned through all its glycogen stores in your liver and muscles. For most of us, if we don't refuel with carbohydrates, we'll run out around 20 miles (32 km) or two hours into a run.

Even during shorter runs, you can feel extremely fatigued if you haven't fueled adequately. While it's impossible to take in enough calories to replace all the energy you're burning while you're running, you can consume enough to ward off the dreaded wall. In general, I advise runners not to worry about fueling with nutritional products until they hit about an hour of running, and then every 45–60 minutes thereafter. For instance, if you're going out for a two-hour long run in preparation for a marathon, you might take a gel at an hour into the run and then again 45 minutes after that. When it comes down to it, though, we all absorb carbohydrates at different rates and what works to keep one runner up and running will just lead to stomach upset for another. Be sure to experiment with this in training to find what works for you.

Once you've ruled out the possibility of overtraining syndrome, illnesses, fueling mistakes, or the like, you may determine that the strong pull to quit is just your inner chimp putting pressure on your inner wimp to hang it up. That's right, you're being hustled by your brain's gray matter, which is signaling the need to cease running far sooner than your body actually requires. And if you don't resist those demands and stick around to withstand a bit of calculated stress, sometimes referred to as cumulative fatigue, you'll never improve.

When I interviewed South African professor of exercise and sports science and the author of *Lore of Running*, Tim Noakes, for a 2009 *Running Times* magazine story, he insisted, "If you want to be competitive, you have to learn how to deal with the discomfort. A lot of the heavy, good physical training is about training the brain to cope with discomfort." More recently, Hecht echoed that point, telling me that "mindfulness may help you work with discomfort and fatigue and push through it."

The nature of fatigue, whether it's mental or physical, is an ongoing debate. Noakes' Central Governor Theory is always referenced in this discussion. He posits that the muscles and other organs transmit signals to the brain to help it determine when you're tired, presenting a kill-switch of sorts that your brain employs if you are nearing dangerous levels of fatigue. Think of the thermostat in your house. It automatically pumps out warm or cool air in order to maintain a certain temperature. In the same way, Noakes suggests that your body subconsciously regulates effort and fatigue to bring you back to homeostasis.

"The brain is there to look after you and to make sure whatever you do, you do it safely," Noakes told me, saying that our brains keep us from pushing past a certain point. "There's a control mechanism to make sure that you reach the finish line not in a completely, utterly wilted state. You always have a little reserve."

Recent research by exercise physiologist Samuele Marcora at the University of Kent in Canterbury, UK, offers a twist on this hypothesis, what he calls the "psychobiological model." The Italian-born exercise physiologist has led the charge in asserting that when it comes to endurance sports, fatigue is a psychological construct—that even the toughest athletes have a limit to how much energy they're willing to expend, at which point they quit.

To be sure, researchers have struggled to pinpoint any one physiological parameter that reliably causes fatigue, so perhaps it is all in our heads. The most likely explanation, though, is that it's a multifactorial phenomenon—a complicated interaction between body and brain. Exercise physiologist and coach Steve Magness told me:

"I don't think we have all the answers yet. The way I look at it is that effort and pain are feedback—your body's way of telling you that what you're doing is starting to get hard and it's putting you outside of your homeostasis. That's not a bad thing, it's just your body signaling you. If you continue to push further outside your comfort zone, the signals will become more intense because it's your body's goal to drag you back to that norm value."

Exercise 4.3: If you're out for a run and you begin feeling worn out, try picking up the pace for 50 steps to wake up your system. Count each step left-right-left as you drive your knees and surge forward. After 50 paces, settle back into your original pace.

Magness tells athletes that they can take solace in the fact that unless something is medically wrong, you're typically not going to be able to push so hard that you end up hurting yourself. So while you may feel like you're going to die as you sprint into the finish of a race, you aren't. "It's about knowing what those signals of effort mean and coming to terms and accepting them, thinking, 'Okay, this is going to hurt, but I'm going to accept it and do the best I can in the moment,'" he added.

Next time you're on a run and you become aware of fatigue, mindfully stay with the sensations of your tired legs as you plod up a steep hill and that intense desire to quit. Similar to the mindful strategies for battling pain on the run, fighting fatigue is often an exercise in simply noticing and labeling. Fathoming how things are in the moment also keeps you from catastrophizing and worrying about getting through the miles down the road.

Fortunately for runners, mindfulness training has been shown to reduce fatigue. Coupled with the knowledge that exercise boosts energy levels and fights lethargy in the long run—even more effectively than using stimulant medications—mindful running's potential to produce a calm and highly energetic body and brain is profound.

Action Items

- In your head, label the physical sensations and emotions you notice.
- If you suspect the exhaustion is a symptom of overtraining, take a few days off from running and rest up. Consider adjusting your training plan.
- If you're under-fueled, cut the run short and head home for a big meal. Reevaluate your nutritional strategy.
- If the discomfort is related to the inherent fatigue associated with exercise, stay with it for a moment.
- Try to avoid getting sidetracked by judging the sensations as good, bad, pleasant, or unpleasant. Simply notice and accept.
- As you put some distance between the feeling and the thought, remind yourself that in the long run, exercise will give you more energy, rather than sapping it.
- Shift your thinking to a different object of your attention in the present moment—the terrain underfoot or the rhythmic sound of your breath.
- Again, a positive mantra may come in handy here to help get you through "the wall." Choose a motivating word or phrase to repeat in your head.

Stress: Getting Hijacked

It was the third and final round of the women's 1,500-meter race at the 2000 Olympics in Sydney, Australia and expectations for 32-year-old American Suzy Favor Hamilton were colossal. The three-time Olympian was ranked number one in the world and was just the second American woman in history to crack the four-minute barrier in the 1,500. The 5-foot-3, slender, blonde phenom stood on the starting line intensely focused through her blue-lensed sunglasses. When the gun fired, she almost immediately took the lead—an ambitious tactical choice for the seasoned runner. As the race unfolded, there was some jockeying for the top positions, but Favor Hamilton managed to hang with the lead pack and remained in contention for the win.

Then something wholly unexpected happened. Maybe it was the flashbulbs popping around the Olympic oval and the 120,000 screaming fans. Or perhaps it was the pressure to win an Olympic gold after coming up short at her two previous appearances at the Games. It could have even been the burden of a number of big-budget sponsorships and promotional deals weighing on her. Regardless of the catalyst, after retaking the lead at the outset of the bell lap, one, two, three, four runners powered past her on the home stretch. Suddenly out of medal contention, she stiffened up and dramatically flopped down on the track.

In her 2015 memoir, *Fast Girl: A Life Spent Running from Madness*, she explained that in a moment of panic and sheer dread at the thought of running another step, she purposely fell. Under the weight of winning expectations, stress and anxiety took over. In her book, she wrote of the dread she felt at the thought of disappointing anyone, which paradoxically, was what led to her downfall.

While most of us don't get the opportunity to falter on such a public stage, nearby everyone has experienced choking under pressure at one time or another. Our hectic and fragmented world pretty much requires that we schlep around this type of toxic emotional baggage. Fathoming these feelings is not always pleasant, but it's necessary. A 2016 study published in the *Journal of Research in Personality* suggests that people with a more adept sense of present-moment awareness also have far better coping skills when it comes to stress. Not only do mindful people respond to stressful situations by employing more effective strategies that boost health and well-being, they also bounce back more quickly.

If you observed feelings of stress and anxiety in Step One, it is likely connected to mind wandering. You might be on a run where you find yourself endlessly deliberating about that presentation you have to give at work, a disagreement you had with a friend, or a tough lecture you need to dispense to your child. While running can provide optimal grounds to work through many of these issues, when we leave the brain to its own devices, it becomes a practice in rumination rather than resolution.

In *The Book of Joy*, Douglas Carlton Abrams chronicles a week-long meeting between Nobel Peace Prize Laureates His Holiness the Dalai Lama and Archbishop Desmond Tutu, during which they explored the true nature of joy and the many obstacles to it. I wholeheartedly identified with one simple line from that book where it is suggested that we often manufacture unnecessary stress in our lives by "wanting things to be different than they are."

When I'm being mindful, I notice anxious thoughts and can make a deliberate decision about what to do next, if anything. While we can't eliminate the stresses that inherently accompany daily life, we can step back and ask ourselves, "Is having this predictable track of worries on repeat productive? Am I making a difficult situation worse by trying to ignore or resist feelings?"

Consider the case of champion track cyclist and six-time gold medalist Sir Chris Hoy of Great Britain. His battle with pre-race panic attacks has been widely covered. Paralyzed by the pressure to perform every time he entered the velodrome, his heart would race and palms sweat as he found himself repeatedly enshrouded in doom and dread prior to competition. Bearing the cross of national hero and global inspiration, his brain would shift into fight-or-flight mode. To address these feelings, he worked with Steve Peters, the author of *The Chimp Paradox*, who taught him how to tame his "inner chimp" by being more mindful. In learning to focus in on the emotions instead of fighting them, he was able to rationalize instead of catastrophize, thereby overcoming those intrusive thoughts and emotions.

Most of us are under far less competitive pressure than Hoy or Favor Hamilton, but we all have moments when we feel overwhelmed. No matter where your stress is rooted, there's plenty of research to show how heavy-handed anxiety can be when it comes to hampering running performance. Increased heart rate, intestinal distress, lack of focus, decreased immunity, and poor sleep are all by-products of stress and anxiety. What's more, these emotions put your body in a constant state of tension and guardedness. When your muscles stiffen up, not only do you expend more energy, your motor patterns change. This results in a less-than-optimal stride pattern.

Coach Lucy Smith, a 19-time Canadian champion in running and duathlon who has come to embrace the ethos of mindfulness, teaches these principles to other runners. When I spoke to her, she told me:

> **Pro Tip:** If you're feeling tense and tight on account of stress, drop your hands and shake your arms out a couple of times as you're running. This is like hitting the reset button to release tension and relax.

"If you're not being mindful, there's a good chance you're carrying stress or tension without knowing it, which is going to physiologically prevent you from maximizing

*your potential. Mindfulness teaches you to pay attention
to whether your shoulders, neck, and jaw are relaxed
and whether your posture is nice and tall. When you stay
relaxed, you run better because your muscles naturally
work better when they aren't carrying tension. This also
helps head off injuries."*

In the same way that there is good and bad pain and fatigue, there is positive and negative stress, often called eustress and distress. A calculated amount of stress has been shown to create "optimal arousal" in athletes. In the world of psychology, this is known as the Yerkes-Dodson Law. Posited by psychologists Robert Yerkes and John Dillingham Dodson in 1908, they discovered that by administering mild electric shocks to rats when they incorrectly navigated a maze, they could motivate them to learn how to make it through the puzzle more quickly.

But that only worked to a point. Once the jolts reached a certain voltage, the rats' performance suffered. Imagine an inverted "U," also known as "the zone of optimal functioning." The bottom of the left side of the arch represents no stress and therefore a sense of malaise or lethargy. It's when you aren't at all engaged in what you're doing.

As you travel up to the top of the curve, you hit the sweet spot of optimal stress—the point where your brain triggers a release of chemicals, like dopamine, cortisol and adrenaline. In small amounts, this cocktail helps put you in the range of good stress, whether that helps you pick up the pace in a workout or push through a deadline at work. When the stress hormone levels get too high, however, you enter the bottom right side of the curve and performance suffers. Think back to the example of the Jitter Jar—when your system is awash in stress hormones, the jar is a tempest of glitter. Imbalances arise in the nervous system and we feel off-kilter and unable to think clearly or perform with precision. It's the difference between being psyched up and psyched out.

Mindfulness guides you to notice the true source of stress, slow down anxiety's chaotic roll call, accept worries without judgment, and then refocus on more useful thinking. When I catch stress and anxiety snowballing, I practice what I call "PAUSE."

> **P:** Pause your mental dialogue for a moment and notice the specific thoughts that are going through your mind.
>
> **A:** Accept your thoughts and the situation in that moment.
>
> **U:** Understand the emotions that are connected to the thoughts.
>
> **S:** Strategize your next step. If you deem the line of thinking isn't productive, come up with a plan to slow down and bring calm to your body and mind.
>
> **E:** Execute your chosen plan of attack.

As the cyclist Hoy discovered, noticing unproductive anxieties is the first step to reducing their power. Since many of us live in an almost constant state of stress, recognizing those emotions, as well as the physiological consequences, usually takes some work. Similar to the strategy of labeling a thought, Sian Beilock's work at the Human Performance Laboratory at the University of Chicago has found that journaling about anxieties related to completing a stressful task can improve subsequent performance by 15 percent.

Exercise 4.4: In your training journal, write down the worries that are running through your head. Whether they are about finishing a project at work, relationship troubles, or an unexpected hiccup in your training, list them as they come to mind. Try doing this at least once a week.

Reframing anxiety as excitement can additionally mitigate some of the less desirable effects of stress in performance scenarios. Say you're standing at the starting line of a race and you're fathoming stomach-churning pre-race nerves. Research from Harvard Business School suggests that instead of interpreting anxious thoughts in your mind with an impending sense of doom, consider that those jitters may just be part of the inherent buzz that is associated with tackling a new challenge. To be sure, psychotherapy studies have found that we have the power to edit and reinterpret our inner dialogue, which can give you a greater feeling of control.

Whatever approach you choose, Raoul Oudejans' work in Human Movement Sciences at the VU University Amsterdam has highlighted the importance of practicing under high-pressure conditions if you hope to perform when it counts. While you can't 100 percent mimic a competitive scenario in training, moderate amounts of stress in workouts can boost body and brain function optimally when you toe the line on race day. Key workouts that test not only physical speed, strength, and endurance but also your mental faculties, like the weekly long run in a marathon training program, can help prep you for competition.

Action Items

- Identify and label the physical sensations and emotions that are related to stress and anxiety.
- Decouple stressful cognitions about life and running. Stay with the thoughts for a moment and figure out whether or not the line of thought is productive.
- If you notice that the same anxious thoughts are recycling through your head over and over, interrupt that process by labeling and accepting them without judgement.
- Get the stress off your chest by writing about it in your training journal after a run.

- As you put some distance between the feelings and the thoughts, notice how your body responds. Do you feel your shoulders relax or tension release from your jaw and forehead?
- Remember, some level of stress is normal in training and it serves an important purpose. Exist with your nerves and reframe them as excitement to fuel the competitive fire.

Negative Self Talk: The Devil on Your Shoulder

Gale-force crosswinds reaching speeds of 25 miles per hour, gusted a squall of horizontal rain across the Oxford University Iffley Road track on 6 May 1954. The blustery day was not the one Roger Bannister had envisioned for his effort to break the four-minute mile. Already a purportedly impossible feat, he knew the whipping wind and rain would slow him close to a second per lap so he'd have to put in closer to a 3 minute 56 second effort. Nevertheless, the 25-year-old medical student finished his rounds that morning and proceeded to sharpen his spikes on a grindstone at the St Mary's Hospital Medical School laboratory in preparation for the endeavor.

When he arrived at the track, the wind mercilessly lashed a rain-soaked English flag hanging on an adjacent church steeple. Bannister couldn't help but notice, questioning whether the attempt should be put off. Eventually the powerful gusts slowed to a breeze and at 6.00 p.m., Bannister and the others toed the line. His freshly honed spikes dug into the cinder track made of discarded ash from the local power stations as he waited pensively under overcast skies for the gun to fire.

Back in the 1950s, the barrier du jour was the four-minute mile. At the time, hordes of experts agreed that it was physiologically impossible and men would die trying to go under the mark. As a doctor and physiologist in training, Bannister remained steadfast in his belief that it was attainable. And he wasn't alone. Two other men were chasing the record at the time and inching closer with each effort: Australian John Landy and American Wes Santee.

The repeated attempts to break the elusive barrier were followed by people all over the world, stealing headlines from the conclusion of the Korean War and the escalating arms race between the U.S.S.R. and the United States. Coupled with Sir Edmund Hillary's successful climb to the summit of Everest in May 1953, the possibility of a man running a sub-four-minute mile inspired people to think beyond perceived human limits.

When the runners at the Iffley Road track jumped from the starting line that wet and windy day in May, one of Bannister's pacers immediately went to the front, leading the runners through the first quarter mile in 57.5 seconds. By the halfway point, they were at 1 minute 58 seconds. Bannister urged himself to relax into the pace—not to get overzealous with two laps to go. His pacers took him through three-quarters of a mile in 3 minutes 7 seconds. Around 1,500 fans in overcoats and felt trilby hats white-knuckled their stopwatches, urging on the long-legged Bannister as he swung around the last turn, charged into the homestretch, and leapt at the tape.

Collapsing onto the cinder track, he wrote in his 1980 book, *The First Four Minutes*, that he felt "like an exploded flashlight." Fans eagerly awaited the final time to be announced. The announcer didn't get past declaring "three minutes ..." before he was drowned out by the Oxford crowd erupting in celebration. 3:59.4. The Englishman had done the impossible.

Bannister's spectacular accomplishment leaves one to wonder what made him special. After numerous attempts over the years by countless runners, why was he the one to finally do it? The simple answer is self-belief. He pushed back on supposed experts who declared it impossible and didn't get caught up in a negative inner narrative. While his competitor Landy felt he had hit a wall after running 4 minutes 2 seconds or better on six separate occasions between 1952 and 1954, he deemed it an unreachable mark. Bannister, however, never lost faith in his own abilities.

The first sub-four-minute mile illustrates how vital it is not to allow self-criticism and self-doubt to cut short your ambitions. Indeed, a little over six weeks later, Landy crushed a 3 minute 58 second mile. Today, countless men have run under four minutes. Even more impressive, the record has been lowered by almost 17 seconds since then, run by Morocco's Hicham El Guerrouj.

This phenomenon is sometimes referred to as the "Bannister Effect." It is the idea that once someone sees that something seemingly impossible is possible, they are then able to achieve it. How many of us harbor beliefs about our identities and abilities that place limits on our achievements?

It's perfectly normal if you noticed self-defeating thoughts running through your head in Step One. We humans tend to sell ourselves short. Mindfulness sheds light on those thoughts of which you may not have even been aware. Similar to the way stress and anxiety tend to get out of hand when we are operating in autopilot, so can our inner critic. Here are some of the most common types of negative self-talk:

- Self-criticism: "I'm too fat to be a runner." "I'm not at all athletic." "I'm in terrible shape."
- Self-doubt: "I'll never be able to hit that pace." "I'm not going to be able to run that far." "I don't have the right body type to ever be a good runner."
- Self-pity: "I always get stuck at the back of the pack in races." "I have the worst luck with weather conditions on race day!"

Not only has negative self-talk been shown to be an impediment to achieving flow, it can also be a self-fulfilling prophesy. Perhaps you weren't initially the slowest runner in your running group until your inner critic began insisting you were. What's more, research out of Bangor University in the UK has shown that motivational self-talk and visualization can have the opposite effect by enhancing endurance outcomes.

Exercise 4.5: When Spanish researchers had people write down on a piece of paper something they disliked about their body, instructed half of them to throw away the paper and the other half to keep the paper, and then later had them all rate their body image on a scale, those who threw the thought away reported a higher opinion of themselves. It was as if they discarded the thought in the same way they threw away the paper with the thought written on it. If you tend to be hard on yourself, give this technique a try.

***

Self-compassion is an essential pillar of any mindfulness practice and it plays a big role in helping you deal with negative self-talk. Emma Seppälä, the science director of the Center for Compassion and Altruism Research and Education at Stanford University and author of *The Happiness Track*, suggests that self-compassion can be learned by treating yourself the same way you would a good friend. This is a type of "Socratic questioning," which has been shown to reduce depressive thinking because it forces you to consider the validity of negative thinking, thereby prompting a broader perspective.

For example, if your running buddy fell far short of their goal in a race, would you say: "What's wrong with you? You're such a failure!" or "Don't worry about the race. You did the best you could today." Which of these sounds closer to the way you talk to yourself? If it's the former, rather than the latter, you could stand to treat yourself with a bit more compassion.

Exercise 4.6: Take a moment to visualize the runner you want to be. Imagine yourself running with perfect form and drive. What does that look, feel, and sound like? If you find that you lack self-belief, try employing this strategy before your run each day until it's ingrained in your mind.

The mindful approach doesn't involve trying to eradicate these thoughts, but rather to rewire your response to them in an effort to avoid fueling the fire of negativity. Here are some examples of how to respond when that judgmental voice inside your head gets going:

- Instead of "I suck at running. I'm so slow."
- Think: "I'm building fitness every day I get out there to train. Patience is a virtue."
- Instead of "I'm not a runner and I'm not fooling anyone. This is so embarrassing."
- Think: "I'm doing something good for my body and mind and no one can judge me for that."

Research conducted at the Institute for the Psychology of Elite Performance at Bangor University in the UK has also demonstrated that having a few practiced positive statements in your psychological skills' arsenal can help reduce how hard aerobic exercise feels, thereby boosting performance. Just as negative self-talk can lead to self-fulfilling prophesies, so can positive affirmations.

Exercise 4.7: In your training journal, write down three motivating statements that you can draw upon during a challenging moment on a run. The UK study used statements like "feeling good" and "going strong," but be sure to choose something that works for you. Once you come up with a few you're happy with, begin to practice them when you're running.

One final method by which many athletes battle negative self-talk is simply to look back at the training they've done and use it as evidence to prove their inner critic wrong. Self-efficacy is defined as the belief you have in your abilities. Again and again in the sports psychology literature, an athlete's sense of self-efficacy in their sport has proven to be linked to performance. Unsurprisingly, when researchers at the Catholic University of America in Washington D.C. put athletes through mindfulness training, they discovered a boost in their self-confidence. It is only when you lose touch with your cognitions that they serve to trick you into thinking you aren't capable of certain achievements.

* * *

Janet Cherobon-Bawcom knows a whole lot about cultivating self-belief. Back in 2013, I was working on a profile of the 2012 Olympian in the 10,000 meters and 2 hour 29 minute-marathoner, leading up to the New York City Marathon for espnW. Now a U.S. citizen, she grew up the oldest of eight children to a single mother in the village of Kapsabet, in the former Rift Valley Province of Kenya. At 19 years old, she was walking along a dusty roadway, making the 40-mile trek on foot to visit an aunt in Eldoret, when she was spotted by a local coach who just happened to be driving by. He quickly sized her up and suggested she might be a good runner.

The coach, as it turned out, was a reasonable person to be making such snap judgments. He happened to be Peter Rono, a 1988 Olympic champion in the 1,500 meters. Amused at the thought of this memory, Cherobon-Bawcom laughed, telling me she didn't know who Rono was and at the time all she could think was, "I'm not a runner, you're talking to the wrong person."

Just six months later, she happened upon Rono again along another dusty roadside in Kapsabet. Thanks to his continued insistence, she eventually decided to give running a try. It took some time to build up her fitness, but soon the Kenyan farm girl caught the eye of coaches at Harding University in Arkansas, who offered her a scholarship to run. Just a couple years earlier, she had no ambitions to attend a university 10,000 miles from home, much less run in the NCAA. She was too busy helping her mother take care of her brothers and sisters in between tending to the family farm's goats and cows.

She literally had to build her system of self-belief from the ground up to shape her running identity. The way she did this was to approach each day of training as a brick in the foundation of her confidence. When I asked her what she thought about during races, she told me:

> "My positive self-talk is usually me flashing back to the training I've done — the workouts that went well and showed me that I'm ready to accomplish whatever the day's task is. If I've got a tough 2-mile stretch in a race, I'll think back to a great 2-mile repeat at Buffalo Park in Flagstaff and I'll remind myself, 'I've done this in practice, so just do it again out here on race day.'"

There are a few different ways to gather performance feedback to boost self-belief as Cherobon-Bawcom did. Data from a smartphone or smartwatch can provide you with information on the mileage and training paces you've logged over the course of a season. Similarly, a written training log is another way to chronicle the workouts you've successfully completed, to look back on in moments of doubt. "Check-in" workouts are yet a third way to track your progress. This could be a time trial or interval workout you do once a month to see tangible improvements in your speed, strength, and endurance.

Action Items

- Identify and label the statements of your inner critic.
- Notice how your body responds to these thoughts. Does it make you feel tense? Fatigued? Anxious?

- Work on reinterpreting these thoughts and mindfully reframing them as motivational statements.
- Write down the negative self-talk and come up with new statements to replace them.
- Begin a running log to track your progress to build a better sense of self-efficacy.

Boredom: Embracing Ennui

Danish philosopher Søren Kierkegaard called it the root of all evil and he's not the only one to espouse those sentiments. Boredom definitely has a bad reputation. We overschedule our children in organized sports and after-school activities and pack our days with work, meetings, errands, and social engagements, making time alone with our thoughts rare. We are constantly hopscotching from one distraction to the next, even filling small gaps of time tooling around on our smartphones.

If you need proof of how much humans loathe boredom, consider a recent study in which researchers from the University of Virginia sequestered students in a small, austere room and instructed them to sit at a table and be alone with their thoughts for 15 minutes. The only form of entertainment was a small button, which, if pressed, would deliver an electric shock to their ankle. It turned out that, rather than sit in solitude and do nothing, the 15 minutes of tedium led 67 percent of men and 25 percent of women to shock themselves. To be clear, the majority of participants chose a sharp zap to the ankle over simply sitting quietly and contemplating their own cognitions.

Running, by nature, is repetitious. Put one foot in front of the other. Repeat. That's probably why boredom is one of the top reasons people cite for hating the sport. Mindfulness provides an antidote to feelings of boredom on the run. By focusing on and getting familiar with boredom, the frenetic pace by which we operate slows and we push back against the impulse to flee from our own thoughts and emotions. Mindful running calls you to peel back the layers of the mind to discover what software is running in the background of your operating system. Quite often, you'll find the scene isn't the least bit boring.

Exercise 4.8: If you're a big user of gadgetry to eschew the boredom of the run, try scheduling one run a week without any technology. Ditch the music, the GPS watch, the heart-rate monitor, and even your phone. Also, choose a new route to help you wake up and pay greater attention to the novelty of the run.

When I was speaking to "Ultramarathon Man" Karnazes recently, I asked him how he dealt with boredom on, say, a 350-mile run. "Running can be really boring, but boring is good," he told me. "I think people need to shift their paradigm of boring. We often feel like we have to always occupy our time. I think running can really be a vacation for the mind."

Spend a moment fathoming the origins of your ennui. Is running really all that boring or are you just so accustomed to constant distraction that you're having trouble being alone with your own thoughts? Mindfully staying with the feeling and seeing it for what it is can segue into ease in both body and mind. Plus, you might even discover that things as they are in the present moment are far more noteworthy than you originally thought.

When I asked Alexi Pappas how she works with boredom while racing 25 laps around a 400-meter track in a 10,000-meter race, she referred to her mindfulness practice and the importance of staying curious about the things she notices in the moment. "I never get bored," she told me. "I count laps and try to watch myself running the race as I'm running it—to almost amuse myself while everything is unfolding." This mindset leads to more relaxed running with better regulation of pace, effort, posture, and form.

Tune In: Learning to bring curiosity to your body and brain takes some practice. Try this: Sit back and close your eyes for a moment. Bring your attention to your feet with a mind of curiosity. Become aware of the tops of your feet and then the soles. Do they feel tight, warm, cold, achy, or relaxed? Bring your attention to each individual toe on your left foot and then your right foot. Are they tingling, sore, or do you feel nothing at all? Try this exercise again tomorrow—you'll see how the sensations change from one day to the next.

If you're regularly observing feelings of boredom on the run, it may be time to take some action to boost your curiosity quotient to remedy the languor. While many runners get in a rut running the same mileage, pace, and route day after day, research shows that mixing up the types of workouts you do, as well as the routes you run, can help mitigate boredom and keep you engaged. This may mean logging a speed session on the track or doing a long run on a new set of trails to keep things interesting. Indeed, a Canadian study found that people actually tended to enjoy high-intensity training more than moderate workouts. Strategically placed high-intensity sessions can be something to look forward to, rather than dread.

Action Items

- Identify and label the feelings of boredom.
- Take note of how boredom affects your running pace and posture.
- Determine whether your boredom springs from an internal struggle to be alone with your thoughts or if there are

some simple things you could do to make your runs more interesting.

- If you're simply avoiding existing with your thoughts and emotions, tune in to those feelings and label what you observe.
- If you determine that some action needs to be taken in order to better engage your mind, consider changing up your workouts, pace, or route.

Attachment: Clinging, Craving, and Hoarding

In Robert Pirsig's oddball 1974 novel, *Zen and the Art of Motorcycle Maintenance*, he describes the "South Indian Monkey Trap." This method of monkey trapping involves cutting a small hole in one end of a hollow coconut and placing rice inside to entice a hungry monkey. The coconut is then chained to a stake in the ground. When the monkey approaches and inevitably sticks his hand in to retrieve the rice, he can't pull it out as long as his fist is clenched around the loot. The only way to free himself is to let go.

Not all the thoughts you notice in Step One will be negative. Some may be wholly pleasurable to ponder. Perhaps you found yourself daydreaming about that perfect date you went on last night or maybe your mind is dominated by anticipatory thoughts involving an upcoming birthday or anniversary. I often catch myself fixating on a work project I'm excited about or even that bottle of wine I plan on opening with my husband at the end of the day.

Unfortunately, when that thinking gets out of hand, it can be like the reality series about hoarders. People on the show get so attached to certain things that they accumulate junk in their homes from floor to ceiling until they are nearly buried alive. Similarly, we waste a huge amount of mental energy compulsively craving or clinging to certain, thoughts, emotions, and experiences. It's as if we can't just enjoy something in the moment because we are so afraid of losing it. This can end up triggering stress and anxiety, making it a terrible distraction when we should be focusing on what's directly in front of us.

Exercise 4.9: Moment of Gratitude: If you find you're clinging to particular memories, emotions, or experiences, spend a moment reflecting on three things you're grateful for in the present. Write them down in your training journal and then try to let them float from your mind. Think of it like a to-do list—once you write it down, you can let it go.

The idea of nonattachment is one of the basic tenets of mindfulness. The more pleasant cousin of rumination, clinging to certain thoughts keeps us from living in the moment. Learning to mindfully engage in this type of thinking at appropriate times, and to notice and release these thoughts at other times, is a skill that can be achieved by training the brain through mindfulness. Understanding that everything is impermanent allows you to appreciate the memory or feelings without getting caught up on them.

Research conducted at the Center for Mind and Brain at the University of California, Davis found that nonattachment contributes to psychological well-being. Another study identified an inverse association between nonattachment and depression. The widely held conclusion reached in the nonattachment literature is that releasing the mind from fixating on thoughts and emotions, both pleasant and unpleasant, frees it up for healthier, more objective thinking in the present.

Action Items

- Identify and label the feelings and thoughts.
- Take note of how these thoughts affect your body as you run. Is your stride or pace different than usual?
- Exist with those feelings for a moment.

- Take a moment to feel grateful for the pleasant thoughts or emotions.
- Instead of clinging to the thoughts, write them down in your training journal and let them go.

Brainstorming: Adjusting Your Weathervane

There's good reason that running is often cited as a platform for creativity. Literary icons like Haruki Murakami, Joyce Carol Oates, and Louisa May Alcott have written of the similarities between writing and running, citing repetition, rhythm, self-discipline, and focus. Time spent logging miles serves as an opportunity to reset, ponder projects and problems, and come up with unique solutions.

Even the most accomplished Buddhists aren't engaged in mindfulness 100 percent of the time. Research conducted at the University of Aberdeen in Scotland suggests that our attention tends to naturally ebb and flow, no matter how hard we may try to sustain focus. Studies in the field of cognitive neuroscience have zeroed in on several positive elements of mind wandering. First and foremost, some amount of daydreaming has been shown to be associated with working memory, which is a key player in allowing us to think about several things at a time. In effect, daydreaming trains our brains to juggle multiple thoughts at once. Other research out of the University of California, Santa Barbara demonstrated that mind wandering boosted a person's ability to come up with creative solutions to problems.

The key here is to embrace the seemingly paradoxical philosophy of mindful mind wandering. Being mindful in regards to brainstorming and daydreaming simply involves deliberately choosing to direct your thoughts in a certain way. Think of it like a weathervane for your cognitions. Check the direction of the arrow in order to determine which way the wind is blowing. If the daydreams are gusting in a useful direction, working out a creative solution for instance, continue letting those ideas flow. If, however, your mind's barometric pressure is dropping and a storm of ruminative thoughts are moving in, it's time to readjust and pull yourself out of mind-wandering mode.

Mindfulness helps train your brain to be more intentional in the thoughts you choose to entertain and those you let float on through your mind's sky. When you aren't able to regulate your daydreaming effectively, your mind can meander to places that are far less pleasant than the present moment. It is at this point that daydreaming goes from dynamic to detrimental.

Action Items

- Interrupt your wandering mind and label your thoughts and feelings in the moment.
- Ask yourself if your cognitions are productive. Are they leaning toward the negative and making your body tense up? Or are they making you feel inspired and light on your feet?
- If it is the former scenario, work on allowing those thoughts to pass through your mind as you redirect your thinking to the present moment.
- If it is the latter scenario, deliberately decide if it's a good time to daydream. If it is, allow those cognitions to flow as you move.

A torrent of thoughts, emotions, and sensations can color the running experience for better or for worse. Focusing on and fathoming the content of your body, mind, and surroundings, and how they interact with one another, leads to a sense of concentrated calm. That heightened state serves as a springboard for entering flow, the magical headspace that is characterized by effortlessness and optimal performance. In the next chapter, you'll learn how mindfulness can help you get there.

CHAPTER 5
STEP THREE: FLOW

"I knew this was going to be a special day as soon as I got out of bed."

THESE WERE THE words of American Olympian Ryan Hall in a press release following the 2011 Boston Marathon. Indeed, the 115th running of the fabled race from Hopkinton to Boston produced the fastest time in history, run by Geoffrey Mutai of Kenya, who finished in 2 hours 3 minutes 2 seconds, almost a full minute ahead of the previous best. What's more, the top four men (including Hall) broke the old course record and Hall's time of 2 hours 4 minutes 58 seconds was the best time ever run by an American (although not certified for American or International records because of the point-to-point nature of the course and the elevation loss from start to finish is too great). Whether it was the strong westerly tailwind that urged the runners along at such a clip or simply the depth in the competitive field that day, no one can say for certain.

Getting to witness this alignment of the running stars on that Marathon Monday in 2011 remains one of the most thrilling events of my reporting career. I spent the beginning part of the race in the press room, located in a hotel ballroom near the finish line, watching the athletes on the big screen, firing off updates via social media, and taking notes for a story. I ran the race back in 2009 and was enjoying a different kind of Boston Marathon experience—one that involved press parties in the evenings instead of early bedtimes and pressure to hit deadlines instead of mile splits.

From the moment the gun fired, Hall took on the role as pacemaker at the front of the pack. He logged a 4 minute 38 second first mile and continued to lead through mile 10. As he loped past the hordes of screaming fans outside Wellesley College around the halfway point, he held his hand to his ear, encouraging cheers. He low-fived fans and fist-pumped, clearly garnering energy from their enthusiasm.

It was about that time I snapped my laptop shut and headed out onto the streets of Beantown to witness what appeared to be a historic race unfolding. If he kept up that blistering pace, his projected finishing time would be around 2 hours 2 minutes 40 seconds. These runners were hoofing it toward a record-breaking day or total disaster. Either way, I wanted to witness it for myself.

It wasn't until mile 19 that the race broke open in dramatic fashion. Mutai surged and his countryman Moses Mosop followed in hot pursuit. Gebre Gebremariam of Ethiopia continued to fight behind him. Hall followed in fourth place. The American said later at the post-race press conference back at the hotel that he was thinking to himself in disbelief, "I am running 2:04 pace and I can't even see the leaders!" Indeed, with a mile to go, Mosop and Mutai were on pace to log the fastest marathon ever run by almost 30 seconds. As they made the final turn onto the homestretch on Boylston Street, it came down to a blistering sprint.

I hustled back to the press area at the finish line to watch Mutai come through. His time prompted conversations about a sub-2:00 hour marathon finally being within reach. Next came Mosop, then Gebremariam, and finally Hall.

In interviews at the finish line, Hall was awestruck. He couldn't fully comprehend or verbalize what had just occurred on the road to Boston. It was as if he had just returned from a spiritual pilgrimage and hadn't yet had time to fully absorb its impact. This sacred headspace he existed in during the race is known as "flow." It's that feeling of being completely present and immersed in relentless forward motion. It's not so much about losing yourself in the run, but being so hyper-focused that nothing else matters but the task at hand. It's that place you go when your motivations are crystal clear, you're completely concentrated on getting the job done, and your mind is free of judgments. Many athletes describe it as being "in the zone."

When I was conferring recently with the now-retired Hall about flow, he described it in an almost transcendent sense. He told me, "When I ran my best races, I wasn't thinking any magical thought or trying particularly harder than any other time. It's when my body is working with me, not against me. It's when I feel my physical body operating at its fullest capacity without having to do anything more than let it run."

Feeling the Flow

You know that visual effect in action movies when a bullet fires out of a gun in slow motion and the camera pans around the protagonist as they demonstrate their supersonic reflexes to dodge the deadly projectile? This illusion is known as "time slice photography" and it perfectly encapsulates what it is like to be in flow. It's that moment when time and space are suspended and you perform and feel at your finest.

Back in the 1970s, Hungarian psychologist Mihaly Csikszent-mihalyi coined the term "flow" to define this "highly focused state of consciousness." Having witnessed the trauma of war growing up in Yugoslavia in the 1930s and 1940s, he became interested in what makes life worth living. He discovered that the origins of happiness lie in partaking in activities that give meaning to our lives and in which we become completely absorbed. He has studied athletes, monks, mountaineers, musicians, and scientists and they all experience flow.

Exercise 5.1: Have you experienced flow? In your training journal, list all the activities in which you've found yourself "in the zone."

In the Zen: From the Mouths of the Pros

Flow can be a tough thing to put into words—nonetheless, I tracked down a handful of Olympic and Paralympic runners around the globe and asked them to try. Here's what they told me:

> *"The flow state is an elevated level of awareness. My mind is totally engaged and everything besides the task at hand is a blur. When I see photos of my races or watch video replays, I sometimes find myself commenting, 'I don't remember that.' For example, on my way to winning the 2014 Boston Marathon, I can't even recall crossing the halfway marker. I was in a state of absolute focus. It's a beautiful thing."*

> Meb Keflezighi, United States, 2000, 2004, 2012, 2016 Olympian, 10,000 meters and Marathon

> *"It is a quasi self-hypnotic state. All external stimuli become meaningless, going unnoticed. Pain seems unable to touch you. Everything remains relaxed and your one goal resonates repeatedly in your mind, 'Let's just keep this going.' Thoughts seem to cease. You are not worried. You do not feel pressure. Even time itself seems to have no bearing on your world."*

> Paul Pollock, Ireland, 2016 Olympian, Marathon

> *"I've found that I best achieve running in the zone during a race or workout when I allow myself to be fully immersed in the moment. Instead of thinking ahead to what I want to do or how I want to feel later in the race, I try to stay*

*present with what is unfolding in that moment. When
I can zone in on the present, I have an easier time blocking
out external distractions, maintaining engagement, and
generally feeling like I am in the flow of the race."*

**Kim Conley, United States, 2012 and 2016
Olympian, 5,000 meters**

*"When I am in the zone there is a control and confidence.
It's a worry-free state, an ability to speed up and slow
down at the drop of a dime, read a situation in seemingly
slow-motion state, and to visualize things before they have
fully developed. It's a state where you feel like you can't
be stopped and where things are done instinctually or
intuitively with fluidity and laser focus."*

**Mohammed Ahmed, Canada, 2012 and 2016
Olympian, 5,000 and 10,000 meters**

*"An energy overcomes you and adrenaline rushes through
you making you do things that you wouldn't normally
think you could do. The only thing you concentrate on is
yourself, nothing else around you exists in that moment."*

**Rhys Jones, Great Britain, 2012 and 2016
Paralympian, 100 and 200 meters**

*"When I'm running and my mind and body are on the same
page, it feels like I am in complete harmony with myself. It's
a very special feeling—a former coach of mine calls it 'hyper
focus'—I felt it most when I competed in the Olympics."*

Alexi Pappas, Greece, 2016 Olympian, 10,000 meters

*"The flow experience is something I wish I could get
in every major race that I try to peak for. It's a strong
sense of confidence in your ability that is gained from an*

effortless feeling in the race. Flow also negates the fatigue or soreness I normally experience. This phenomenon grows as you become more aware that you are 'in the zone' and on target for a fast time or personal best."

Liam Adams, Australia, 2016 Olympian, Marathon

"I think in the flow state you are just very focused on what you are doing and block out all distractions. Time seems to pass at a different speed, slower in a way, but then also really fast."

Angie Petty, New Zealand, 2016 Olympian, 800 meters

"When I'm in the racing zone, everything around me blurs and my focus only involves what is going on in front of me. This blur is both auditory and visual and I am so in tune with my body that I'm able to hear my breathing and footsteps despite an immense crowd. I am hyper-focused on whatever goal I set for that particular race and a lot of the time, I am able to do things that surprise me."

**Chaz Davis, United States, 2016 Paralympian,
1,500 and 5,000 meters**

"Being in the zone in a race means being totally in the moment, you are only thinking about racing and running. In a short race this is focused on tactics, pushing hard, and tolerating pain. In a marathon, this is more about tuning in to pace and rhythm and maintaining that. Sometimes you also get the effortlessness when you are near a peak in fitness and everything from the training and mental state comes together for a great performance."

**Liz Yelling, Great Britain, 2004 and 2008
Olympian, Marathon**

How Flow Enhances Enjoyment, Performance, and Meaning

Positive psychology often points to flow as one of the basic precepts of a happy life. Csikszentmihalyi explains that the flow experience is autotelic, which means the task is the reward in and of itself. This is why flow is associated with greater running enjoyment. When you're fully immersed in the synchronicity of movement, your working muscles don't hurt, you aren't worried about the numbers on the clock, and you aren't distracted by intrusive thoughts.

As was illustrated by the previous statements by elite runners, flow is something that all high-level athletes identify as vital to success in their chosen craft. As do Navy SEALs, master chefs, skilled artisans, brilliant computer programmers, talented maestros, and top literary minds.

With that said, it doesn't make it off-limits to mere mortals; in fact, you've probably experienced it at some point in your life when you were doing something you loved. I'm nowhere near elite in anything, but I regularly experience flow engaged in a number of activities that I'm passionate about, including writing, running, swimming, skiing, cycling, and even tending to our vegetable garden every summer.

Perhaps most significant is the fact that reaching the flow state imbues an activity with an extraordinary sense of meaning that is wholly separate from happiness. Csikszentmihalyi's research has found that people report higher levels of purpose, meaning, and well-being following time spent in the flow state.

Indeed, he argues that the greatest experiences of our lives don't occur when we're sipping Mai Tais on a beautiful ocean beach or indulging in a perfectly seared filet mignon and a bottle of finely aged cabernet at a fancy restaurant. Rather, they occur, as he writes about in his 1990 book *Flow: The Psychology of Optimal Experience*, when we are in the thick of pursuing a chosen and worthwhile task that challenges us mentally, physically, or both.

It's the difference between what positive psychologists call "hedonic happiness" and "eudaimonic happiness." The former is achieved by avoiding pain and seeking pleasure, while the latter is when you're authentically engaged, body and brain, in a challenging pursuit, achieving personal growth and experiencing a sense of purpose. Research by psychologists Veronika Huta of the University of Ottawa and Richard M. Ryan of the University of Rochester did a nice job of illustrating these differences. For their 2010 study entitled "Pursuing pleasure or virtue: The differential and overlapping well-being benefits of hedonic and eudaimonic motives," they rounded up a group of college students and had them engage in activities that either enhanced meaning or boosted happiness. They instructed them to pursue at least one activity each day for ten days that fulfilled either meaning or happiness, depending on which cohort they were in.

While the meaning group reported doing things like forgiving a friend, helping someone, and studying, the happiness group slept in, indulged in candy, and went shopping. Immediately following the study, the happiness group had more positive and fewer negative feelings, but three months later, the positive feelings dissolved. While the students who engaged in meaningful pursuits for those ten days unsurprisingly rated their lives as more meaningful, they weren't as happy at immediate follow-up. A few months later, however, they reported lower levels of negative moods and felt more "inspired," "part of something greater than myself," "enriched," and "deeply appreciating." Indeed, it seems that the good life may not be found in momentary satisfaction, but rather in activities that give us a sense of purpose and meaning over the long haul.

Exercise 5.2: What are three activities that boost happiness in your life? What are three activities that boost meaning? Write these down in your training journal and put a check mark next to any of the activities during which you have experienced flow.

It is the wholehearted pursuit of eudaimonic happiness via your True North Goals (see page 41) that sets you up to reach that highly coveted flow state. What often comes along with that is greater meaning in your miles and, in turn, optimal performance. Dr. Roberto Benzo, a two-time Ironman athlete and pulmonologist who runs the Mindful Breathing Lab at the Mayo Clinic in Rochester, Minnesota put it to me this way: "Mindfulness is a state of simplicity and sincerity with the present moment—you may have these moments with running, a sense of purpose, in which you feel like you're finding yourself, who you are really made of."

Finding Flow

Reaching that heightened state of consciousness isn't like a switch you can mindlessly turn on and off. As 2004 silver medalist and winner of the 2009 New York City Marathon and 2014 Boston Marathon, Meb Keflezighi, explained to me recently, "Achieving flow doesn't happen with the snap of a finger." He continued saying, "As an athlete I get there through movement. After a period of time, my mind starts to tune out distractions and I slip into that elevated state. Today, with so many years of experience, I can even get there on regular training runs."

It is a mindful approach to your running practice that creates the right conditions for entering this supernatural headspace. Indeed, research published in the *Journal of Clinical Sport Psychology* has demonstrated that as little as a month of mindfulness training can assist athletes in achieving flow. By existing in the present, monitoring thoughts and physical sensations, and fully engaging in forward motion, you train your brain to cross the Rubicon into that next-level state of mind.

"It starts with an intention to create a mindset that allows flow to happen," Olympian Deena Kastor told me. "Flow can't be forced, because a force is met with a counter force. Flow is something that has to happen without tension or pushing."

Csikszentmihalyi's research has demonstrated that flow is attained when there is balance between the challenge of the activity and the skill of the performer. For instance, as was mentioned in Chapter 4, if you perceive something to be too easy for your skillset, you end up feeling somewhat apathetic (the left side of the inverted "U"). Think of an elite runner who participates in a citizen's race. If she knows there won't be any challengers, she would probably lack the necessary motivation to compete at her best, which would put flow out of reach. If, conversely, the challenge is high and your skillset is low, you would end up feeling quite anxious (the right side of the inverted "U"). Imagine being a new runner thrown into a marathon. Being unprepared or undertrained for an event also prevents flow from being accessible.

In either case, the imbalance between challenge and skill makes the flow state impossible to attain. You want to be right on the top of the curve where your highest strengths meet the challenge at hand. That is exactly where Hall existed that day in 2011 in Boston.

While you've already slipped into a mindful state by focusing and fathoming, this third step calls you to cultivate a higher level of concentration by choosing a mental anchor for your thoughts as you run. The most popular options are your breath or feet, but find what works best for you. Keep in mind that while a few studies have indicated that focusing on automated processes, like your stride or respiration, can be detrimental to performance, mindfully monitoring these things is entirely unique. A meditative mindset keeps you from judging or trying to change anything about what you are focusing on. You invoke your inner observer, rather than your inner critic. That observer is simply curious about paying attention and exploring, not exerting effort to regulate or disparage. Following the in-and-out of your breathing or the left-right-left-right of your footfall helps you avoid losing track of your wandering mind.

The nonjudgment piece is particularly important here because it emphasizes the fact that if you try to conjure up the flow state through sheer force of will, you'll never find it. As Dr. Benzo recently wrote: "Flow, in life, obeys the Laws of Physics: the lower the resistance—to what happens in the here and now—the higher the flow."

Exercise 5.3: Choose Your Anchor

- Breath: Focus on the feeling of cold air entering your nostrils and the warm exhale. Or maybe you'd rather pay attention to the rising and falling of your chest or belly. Be curious about what you notice and the quality of your breath. Follow the breath all the way to its end and observe the quick turnaround as your body takes in another breath.

- Feet: If it's easier for you to tune in to your feet, you can count footfalls or hone in on the feeling of the ground underfoot and how your foot lands, flexes, and pushes off with each step. Again, curiosity is key. Choose a certain element of your foot strike and explore it with nonjudgmental awareness.

While your thoughts will surely veer off course many times, the practice of mindful running only calls you to bring your attention back to that anchor in the present moment every time you notice you are no longer focused on it. "It's not about monitoring your breathing or running technique," Benzo advised me. "It's the ability to pay attention to your anchor without engaging passing thoughts and emotions and every time your mind does wander again, just kindly bring your attention back to your breath or feet again and again."

Remember, this takes practice, so forgive yourself if your mind repeatedly roams. You can take "a million mulligans," as Dan Harris, author of the *New York Times* bestseller *10% Happier*, puts it.

If you do find yourself thinking about the miles down the road, simply label it—"I'm worrying about not being able to finish this run without walking" or "I'm noticing my body tensing up because I'm struggling to stay on pace and getting anxious"—and redirect your mind back to your breath or footfall.

"Being fully present is always my goal," Hall told me, emphasizing the fact that being in the now is a vital precursor to entering flow. "If I'm worried about how many miles ahead I have to go or I'm beating myself up for mistakes I made in the miles I've already run, it never goes well for me. Being present is a lost art in our culture today."

With practice, you'll find the singular focus on your anchor becomes easier, making that magical headspace all the more accessible. You'll know when you've reached that heightened state because the colors are brighter and sounds are more distinct. "Flow happens when you are doing an activity that you embrace wholeheartedly and time goes by and you don't realize it," Dr. Benzo shared with me. You feel relaxed even though you're expending a considerable amount of energy and your mind is free of distracting and unpleasant thoughts as it is entirely engaged in the run.

Action Items

- Experiment with different anchors to see which is easiest for you to pay attention to and remain focused on.
- If you choose your breath, consider whether you'll focus on the air coming in and out of the nostrils, lungs, or belly. Follow each inhale to its end and then follow the entire exhale.
- If you choose your footfall, count each step up to ten, then repeat. Pay attention to where your foot lands on the ground and how it feels when it pushes off.
- When you notice your mind wandering, gently redirect it back to your anchor. Continually bringing your attention back to your breath or footfall will strengthen new neural pathways over time, enhancing your ability to concentrate.
- You'll find that when everything works right, the focus that is achieved by following your breath or footfall can eventually lead you to the flow state.

CHAPTER 6
MINDFUL RACING

"Racing has taught me that many things don't happen without hard work and that no one else is going to do it for you. It has shown me how to tolerate stress and manage it in a healthy way. Life and running are all about balance."

OLYMPIAN LIZ YELLING offered me this response when I inquired about how her prolific racing career has affected her life at large. To be certain she has no shortage of experiences from which to draw. The 2008 Olympic Women's marathon in Beijing is a prime example. Leading up to the race in Beijing, there was much buzz about the extraordinary caliber of the field and the flat and fast course. Weather and air pollution were wild cards, but experts still believed this could end up being one for the history books. British running star Liz Yelling was in the shape of her life, perhaps not vying for gold, but certainly on track for a top-10 finish. She was joined at the start line by the likes of 2004 silver medalist Catherine Ndereba of Kenya and 2004 Bronze medalist Deena Kastor of the U.S., as well as her countrywoman, former training partner, and marathon world record holder, Paula Radcliffe.

A multiple-time national champion in cross-country, Yelling debuted in the marathon distance at the 2003 Berlin Marathon and qualified for a spot on the 2004 Olympic team heading to Athens. The following year she picked up a Commonwealth Games bronze medal in the marathon and in 2007 she broke the highly touted 70-minute barrier in the half-marathon. Then in 2008, she ran a personal best time at the London Marathon, finishing in 2 hours 28 minutes 33 seconds (5 minute 40 second miles). Put modestly, Yelling had plenty of momentum going into the 2008 Games. This, she hoped, would be her moment to shine.

Despite the pedigree of the field, after the starting gun fired, unleashing the runners onto the streets of Beijing, the initial stages of the race could only be described as pedestrian. With temperatures hovering in the low-70°s F (22°C) and humidity at a brutal 88 percent, the runners were strategically holding back in those early miles to conserve energy in preparation for the heat of the day. The result was a massive group of athletes all bunched together.

The 5-foot-8 Yelling quickly found herself boxed into that front pack, her feet catching the other runners ahead and behind her. She surged to the lead where she could settle into her naturally long stride. With near zero wind, she ran there comfortably until about mile 9, when she tucked back into the pack to let someone else do the work up front, a move that proved to be fateful.

At the 10-mile mark, the course suddenly narrowed on the right side of the road and the pack abruptly shifted to the left to avoid smacking into a line of metal gates. Elbows went up and the runners jockeyed for position. In the chaos, Yelling's foot got clipped from behind by one of her competitors. Without time to respond, she went nearly head-first into the tarmac, turning to her side at the last moment to avoid landing flat on her face.

Adrenaline surged through her body, popping her back upright and moving forward in a split second. Watching the race, it was hard not to cringe when she hit the pavement. But when she hurriedly rose and started running again, most onlookers assumed she was unhurt. She herself did too. Soon enough, though, it became clear that wasn't the case. Her arm swelled up, she struggled to breathe normally, and a searing pain radiated from her left side. She gritted her teeth and soldiered on through the race, finishing in a disappointing 26th place.

It turned out that Yelling fractured a rib in the fall and suffered serious bruising. Having competed since the age of nine, and knowing this could be her final Olympic run, one might think this to be a devastating blow. And certainly it was extremely frustrating, but her words not long after reflected a perspective many runners, both elite and recreational, often forget. In a subsequent interview for *The Flying Runner*, a popular online magazine out of the UK, she spoke of the fall and lackluster finish, quipping, "It is just running."

Now retired from competitive athletics and working as a coach, the mother of three says that mindfully weathering disappointments and challenges in her competitive running career, like that shocking fall in 2008, has helped her harness a more level-headed outlook on life. "Running taught me positive reframing and mindfulness—how to manage stress in a positive way and not be fearful of nerves," she told me. "Learning to be in the moment has been great for me as a mother and great for my kids."

For her, embracing the present moment in training and racing helped prepare her for life in ways she could never have anticipated. "Playing with my kids, focusing in on some element of coaching, talking to my clients, listening to friends and family—you have to be in the moment for all of those things," she said. To be sure, when you embrace the process of training and the ups and downs of racing with greater awareness, you garner a wealth of applicable life skills that you might otherwise miss out on.

This chapter covers how you can apply the principles of mindfulness to competitive scenarios. Despite what the stereotypes may have you believe, mindfulness is not incompatible with achievement. As you've probably figured out from the previous chapters, it won't turn you into a zenned-out swami or a super-chill hippie. In fact, many of the most successful athletes in the world would argue that it's essential for optimal performance.

Routine Matters

There's a famous adage in sports psychology that goes something like this: "It's okay to have butterflies in your stomach; the key is to get them to fly in formation." It's perfectly normal to be anxious in the days and hours leading up to a big race. You've invested time and energy into training and you have high hopes for it to pay off. That's not to mention the fact that there's something inherently anxiety-inducing about the race atmosphere.

On a physiological level, the feeling of butterflies in your stomach is your sympathetic nervous system prepping your body for optimal performance. The adrenal glands secrete adrenaline, while blood is pushed to the working muscles and the five senses

A mindful approach to racing helps you get psyched up, instead of psyched out.

are heightened. When you exist on the top of the curve of optimal functioning, a healthy amount of excitement and nervous energy will help you run at your best. As Alexi Pappas says in her film short, *Speed Goggles*, "Nerves mean you care."

We've learned, however, that you can have too much of a good thing. Race settings are rife with potential to set off a runner's fight-or-flight response. A simple anxious thought about the weather can leave you suddenly drenched in sweat, your heart fluttering, and your breathing irregular. Intestinal cramping and muddled thinking often accompany these symptoms. This is obviously among the most terrible states in which to start a race.

Anxiety, nerves, jitters, whatever you want to call it, getting a handle on these emotions is the main reason athletes have pre-race routines. Cindra Kamphoff, a high-performance coach and sport psychology consultant, is an expert on the subject. She told me that runners frequently get caught up worrying about the "what-ifs" before races:

"We often get nervous or anxious because we are worrying about the future or having regrets about the past. We know that before and during a race it's best to focus on the process in the present and not the outcome. The pre-race routine helps you get a handle on that monkey mind swinging from tree to tree."

Studies reveal that a predictable pre-race routine not only quells anxiety, but it also improves subsequent performance. I'm not referring to hocus pocus superstitions, but rather a rehearsed set of actions that help shift your mind into race mode. This can include things like eating the same pre-race meal or listening to the same pump-up music. My breakfast prior to a race almost always consists of oatmeal, peanut butter, and a banana and I always have a playlist handy that I've been listening to in the weeks leading up to the event. Additionally, one of the most essential aspects of my pre-race routine is a quick body scan and diaphragmatic breathing sequence.

Exercise 6.1: Write down the steps you will include in your pre-race routine. Practice this sequence once a week leading up to a big race.

Short breathing exercises have been shown to improve focus and attention, counteract stress, reduce blood pressure, regulate heart rate, and even diminish symptoms associated with irritable bowel syndrome if you're one of those runners who gets a nervous stomach. It also has the power to invoke higher-order thinking in stressful situations and improve your decision-making skills in a race. A fundamental aspect of mindfulness meditation, diaphragmatic breathing, also known as deep breathing or belly breathing, allows for greater oxygen exchange so more oxygen enters the bloodstream.

Exercise 6.2: Take your pulse by placing two fingers on your wrist or neck. Count the number of beats for 30 seconds. Then close your eyes and take 10 slow and deep belly breaths. Check your pulse again. You'll find that your heart rate slowed. What's more, your blood pressure probably dropped, too.

The autonomic nervous system is a major player in our body's stress-response system. It regulates everything from the cardiovascular system, to respiratory functions, to digestion, and the immune system, among other things. These systems communicate back and forth with the brain to maintain the body's homeostasis. If something goes wrong with one of them, warning signals are sent to the brain so it can respond and take necessary action. Since respiration is the only one of these functions that we can readily control, it offers us a portal by which we can send signals to the brain via the breath.

So, if you're feeling nervous and your breathing gets shallow, your brain interprets that as a warning sign to an impending threat. Conversely, if you spend a few moments taking long, deep breaths, it in effect calls off the dogs, recalibrates your nervous system, and tells the brain all is well.

Kabat-Zinn aptly likens the breath to a bridge piling with a strong river current rushing around it. While the rapids may be wild and rough, with undercurrents and dangerous hydraulics, the piling remains calm, steadfast, and grounded in bedrock. Your breath serves as a foundational source of tranquility, even in the high-pressure atmosphere of a race.

The following five-minute body scan and mindful breathing exercise is a great way to slow your respiration and get control of your heart thumping away in your chest before a race. Simply find a place to sit away from the hustle and bustle of the event, if possible, and complete the following steps.

Five-minute Pre-Race Body Scan and Diaphragmatic Breathing Sequence

1. Sit and close your eyes.
2. Relax your muscles in your feet, calves, thighs, and hips.
3. Let go of tension in your stomach and chest.
4. Now try to relax your back, shoulders, and neck.
5. Lastly, bring attention to your jaw and face and release any strain.
6. Place one hand on your diaphragm, just below your ribcage, and the other hand on your chest.

7. Inhale through your nose to the count of five. Feel your breath enter your nose and flow down into your lungs and then your belly.

8. The diaphragm should rise with each inhale, while the chest stays relatively still. If you need an example, observe how a young child naturally breathes. It may take some practice to train your body to recruit the diaphragm because many adults are in the habit of chronically contracting the abdominals and taking more shallow breaths from the chest.

9. Be sure to fully inflate your lungs, feeling your ribcage and abdomen expand and your spine lengthen. You'll know if you're taking a deep enough breath if you can see the hand on your belly rise and fall with each inhalation and exhalation.

10. After taking in that breath, pause for a second or two.

11. Purse your lips and exhale through your mouth to the count of eight. Feel your breath leave your belly first and then your lungs. Don't force the air out, just let it slowly escape as you relax your belly and chest.

12. Focus your mind on being totally present with each breath.

13. If it wanders, just bring it back without worry.

14. When five minutes are up, open your eyes, stand up, shake out your arms and legs, and head out for a warm-up

Mindful Warm-Up

Hopefully, by the time you get to race day, you've been practicing the mindful running process: *focus-fathom-flow*. Your warm-up serves as your chance to *focus* and *fathom* in order to create the right conditions to enter *flow*. A 10–20-minute easy jog following the mindful breathing exercise is the perfect time to do a quick run-through of the first two steps of mindful running.

Warm-Up Jog

- Scan your surroundings: What do you hear, smell, taste, feel, and see? What is the weather like? How do course conditions look?

- Scan your body: Move your attention from your head down to your toes. Focus on whether anything feels tight or sore.

- Scan your mind: How are you feeling today overall? What are the first three thoughts at the top of your mind?

- Determine whether any adjustments need to be made. Perhaps your hamstrings are tight, so you need to do a little extra stretching after the warm-up. Or maybe you notice a negative storyline running through your head that you need to acknowledge and let go.

This quick rundown of the *focus-fathom* routine offers you reassurance that everything is in working order prior to the start of the race. It also centers your mind and prepares you to slip into that coveted state of flow. The final step of your pre-race warm-up routine involves a few drills to raise the body's core temperature and establish motor patterns and muscle recruitment specific to running.

Since we know that traditional stretching, also known as static stretching, can be detrimental to performance when practiced prior to competition, the following dynamic stretching and plyometric drills are a better option. They emphasize good form, posture, and leg turnover and have been shown to improve running economy, so you need less oxygen to run a given pace.

Similar to the way you strengthen certain neural pathways by thinking, reacting and emoting, specific muscles grow depending on how you move and apply load. As such, it's important to train your body to recruit muscle fibers with efficiency and power.

When you are tuned out during runs, it's easy to overlook muscle imbalances and poor motor patterns. What's more, distance runners often inadvertently neglect the fast-twitch muscle fibers by doing a lot of easy to moderate training. These drills call upon those fast-twitch fibers and train optimal muscle recruitment, thereby allowing you to turn your legs over faster and push off harder.

Plyometrics and dynamic stretching have a priming effect by training muscle activation, thereby enhancing your efficiency and reducing your chances of getting injured. Be sure to invoke your powers of mindfulness as you do these so you're paying attention and executing them properly. Just like the other elements of the warm-up, these should be practiced with some regularity so you're well-versed in the routine come race day. These will take 5–10 minutes and they are to be completed on a flat, 50-meter stretch.

Warm-Up Drills

- **Monster Walk** Stand with good posture and your arms stretched out in front of your body with palms facing down. Begin walking forward as you lift your right leg straight out in front of your body, bringing your toes toward your outstretched palms. Once you've planted your right foot, do the same on the left side as you continue forward.

- **Bounding** Bound forward as if exaggerating your running form. Leap with each step and utilize your arms for propulsion and balance.

- **High Knees** With good posture and your arms in running position, begin jogging forward, alternating popping up your knees with each step. Emphasize a quick vertical cadence, rather than fast forward movement.

- **Butt Kicks** Similar to high knees, alternate kicking your heels to your backside. Again, focus on fast cadence.

- **High Skips** In an exaggerated skipping motion, push off the ground with your right foot, bringing your left knee and right arm upward, then alternate sides.

- **Accelerations** Finish this routine with two 50-meter speed drills. Start slowly and gradually reach top speed by the end of the 50-meter stretch. Rest for a couple moments before turning around and going back in the other direction.

Gun Time

You'll often hear coaches advise runners to "control the controllables" on race day. Things that are in your control include your attitude, what you eat and drink, the way you warm up, what you wear, and how scrupulously you tie your shoes. These "controllables" are worth devoting a bit of energy to getting right. It is less productive to offer much bandwidth to ruminating about things that aren't in your jurisdiction, like the weather and the actions of your competitors. You'll need to mindfully respond as best you can during a race, but it's best not to try to anticipate the infinite number of things that can go wrong before the gun even fires.

High-performance coach and sports psychology consultant Cindra Kamphoff told me that she often reminds the athletes she works with: "Peak performance only happens in the present moment." The ethos of mindfulness will guide you in the heat of competition. All you have to do is tune in to your environment, body, and mind, accept things as they are, and work with whatever hand you're dealt on that particular day. Next, we'll go over a few of the most common environmental, physical, and mental concerns runners encounter on race day, as well as how to respond purposefully.

Race Environment

Consider the case of the 2016 U.S. Olympic Marathon Trials in Los Angeles. It was the hottest Trials on record, with temperatures hovering in the mid-70°s F (24°C) and a blazing sun beating down on the runners. Shalane Flanagan, a 2008 bronze medalist in the 10,000 meters and favorite to win, mentioned in the pre-race press conference that she was unfamiliar with running the 26.2-mile event in such heat.

Flanagan's race started in impressive fashion, as one might expect from a two-time Olympian. She ran with a pack of other well-known pros, including the likes of Kara Goucher, Desi Linden, Sara Hall, and Janet Cherobon-Bawcom. Around mile 14 she and her teammate, Amy Cragg, broke away from the field and led convincingly for the next 10 miles.

That's about the time the heat caught up to Flanagan.

She began to stagger and struggle with just 2 miles to go. Visibly in distress as she made her way down Figueroa, the dead-straight 2-mile road that leads to the finish, she later reported to *Runner's World* that she was suffering from chills and dizzy spells. Her ears rang and she couldn't see straight. She was already in the advanced stages of dehydration and fighting mightily to stay upright. With the finish line looming in the distance, Linden went by her, snagging second place. It appeared the third spot on the Olympic team was open for the taking.

Before anyone else could catch her, though, Flanagan managed to collapse across the finish line in third. She was immediately rushed off to the medical tent where she received IV fluids, the first time she'd needed that kind of post-race attention in her long running career. At the top of the list of topics she discussed the next day in interviews was devising a new hydration strategy for the Olympics in Rio, where heat could also be an issue.

Flanagan's dramatic final miles at the Olympic Marathon Trials illustrate how significant and unavoidable hurdles can get unexpectedly thrown in your path on race day. Even when you've been planning every little detail for months, the way she undoubtedly did, Mother Nature or some other unforeseen force can intervene to potentially foil your plans. This is where mindfulness comes in. Not only does mindful running teach you to accept what is, it also offers you flexibility in devising a new plan on the fly.

While you can't plan for every scenario, being mindful of what you are likely to encounter on race day can go a long way in terms of helping you achieve your goals. A few questions about the course to keep in mind:

> **Pro Tip:** Do your homework before race day. Race websites generally provide a good amount of information about the weather, course, and conditions, but also check out blogs or social media posts with first-hand accounts from other athletes who have run the event in the past.

- What is the terrain?
- Is the course susceptible to changes in weather?
- Are there any major hills? If so, where are they?
- Are there any significant changes in elevation?
- What does the final stretch of the race look like?

Mindful Race Strategy

In the same way mindfulness helps you adapt and respond to changing environmental conditions, it can also assist you in making tactical decisions. To run up to your potential, American elite runner and four-time national champion Heather Kampf, also known as the "Queen of the Road Mile," insists that moment-to-moment awareness is crucial in races. While running might look relatively simple, there are many things you must keep tabs on in the midst of competition.

"I might be focusing on running the tangent in my lane on the track, moving toward a perfect position, checking my splits at certain points, evaluating how I feel or how my form is, maintaining a safe distance from other competitors so I don't cause a tumble—the list could go on," Kampf told me.

Keeping your emotions in check can help you mindfully respond to your competitors in constructive ways. "I try not to react too strongly to anything and just keep an optimistic perspective so that I can run exactly as I need to in order to get the outcome I want," she said. When you're looking to perform optimally, you have to be all business, not getting carried away by any one particular thought, emotion, or action of a competitor, no matter how upsetting it might be.

A fitting example comes from a race Kampf ran back in college in 2008, representing the University of Minnesota. Then Heather Dorniden, she lined up for the final heat of the 600-meter event at the Big Ten Indoor Track Championships. The three-lap race started out uneventfully. She ran with focus and intensity, maintaining second position, just within striking distance of first with 200 meters to go.

Then, without warning, she tripped and abruptly smacked face-down onto the track. It was assumed by most people watching that there was no way she could make up for the distance she had lost on her competitors in such a short race. Still, she promptly rose and started running again. As she gained speed, it became clear that winning the heat was still a possibility in her mind. She flew around the curve, picking off one runner, then another and right at the line, another to win the heat in stunning fashion.

The YouTube video of this race has received over 16 million views. Clearly Kampf's ability to readjust in the moment despite less-than-ideal circumstances strikes a chord with people. While a runner can never be totally prepared for something like this, mindfulness trains you to respond in the most productive way possible in the moment.

Listening to Your Body

I first met Amby Burfoot in the summer of 2008 at the U.S. Olympic Trials for Track and Field in Eugene, Oregon, also known as TrackTown USA. The event is held at the University of Oregon's famed Hayward Field—the birthplace of Nike and the hallowed grounds on which the long-haired, mustachioed running rebel-phenom known as Steve Prefontaine made his name. Working on several articles for *Running Times* magazine, I sat in a folding chair at a table next to Burfoot under the hot and humid press tent. A long-time runner early in my journalistic career, I was downright giddy to be in the presence of the editor-at-large for *Runner's World* magazine and the 1968 winner of the Boston Marathon.

I've long admired Burfoot's writing style—a mix between an expert exercise physiologist and a running buddy you'd like to have a beer with after a workout. Burfoot has suggested that in the 21st century, we runners are often over-reliant on fancy running technology. As such, we end up trusting objective data over what he calls the "brain-body." Whether it's achieving efficient pacing or staying adequately hydrated, learning to respond to physical cues on race day is a key part of optimal running performance.

Consider this scenario: If you hit the halfway point of a 10k and your watch says you're slightly slower than your goal pace, should you abide by the urging of the numbers on the screen and speed up? According to Burfoot, the answer lies in your legs and lungs, not the clock. It is at this point that you need to ask yourself, "How am I feeling?" If you say, "Fantastic! Light as a feather!" then by all means, go full speed ahead. However, if you're feeling fatigued, it is important to pay attention to the brain-body signals and stay the course or even slow down in order to make sure you reach the finish line in one piece.

One of the most oft-cited strategic blunders runners make is getting overzealous in the early miles. It's surprisingly easy to get caught up in the excitement of race day and mindlessly abandon your race strategy because you suddenly believe you're in shape to run faster than you've ever run in training. Called the "fly and die" approach, expending too much energy in the beginning of a race almost surely sets the stage for an ugly finish. While a somewhat conservative start often feels categorically criminal when your legs are fresh, there's plenty of evidence to show that, in general, it's the most efficient way to run the majority of races.

Your Racing Mind

Having practiced mindfulness in training, you're prepared for the myriad thoughts and emotions that can arise on race day. There's a good chance that the things you fathomed in workouts will come up in competitive scenarios too. For instance, say the little devil on your shoulder urges you give in to your burning quads and quit at the halfway mark or maybe he lulls you into a lacklusture pace in those painful final miles of a race. Coach Steve Magness calls these "freak out moments." He explained to me:

> *"The tendency is to want to zone out once the race becomes difficult, but you need to be most aware in those moments. It's really easy to think, 'Okay, I'm starting to hurt, so I'm going to slow down.' Being attuned to what the body is telling you allows you to avoid making those split-second decisions, freaking out and backing off when you're hurting."*

Instead of rashly submitting, focusing on the trajectory of your thoughts in the moment creates some space for you to make intentional decisions about what to do next. Mindfulness helps bridge the unconscious primal reactions and the more evolved centers of thought. "A lot of runners really surprise themselves when they bring mindful awareness to pain," added Magness. "It often allows them to have a breakthrough because they actually get close to their physical capacity instead of shying away whenever that initial moment of pain hits."

If you find yourself tempted to give in to that devil on your shoulder, try one of the following exercises. I often suggest these to the runners I coach as ways to reset and refocus.

Exercise 6.3: A technique similar to one that world record marathon holder Paula Radcliffe uses, change up something minor about your stride for 100 steps. You can slacken your arms a little, drive your knees more, or adjust your posture. While you do this, count each step up to 100. When you hit 100, settle back into your natural form and pace. This is meant to wake up your body and brain and retune your racing mindset when you've begun to lose the battle against negative rumination or you're having trouble maintaining intensity and concentration.

Exercise 6.4: Choose a motivating word or phrase that is meaningful to you and write it prominently on your hand. This can be something as simple as "Light and Fast" or "Strong and Tall." If you're religious, it could be a prayer or verse. It could even be the lyrics from a song. The key is to choose something that inspires you. A quick glance at your hand can serve as a small reminder to hang in there in the toughest moments.

Mindful Post-Race Plan

Regardless of whether you performed beautifully or crashed and burned at a race, continuing to mindfully embrace the growth mindset is essential. Mindful running's emphasis on process means that even when you log a personal best, you continue to work toward your True North Goal. After an event, the ethos of mindful running call you to express gratitude, reflect on results, accept things as they are, and shift gears.

Practice Gratitude

You know that feeling of agony when you're struggling up a big hill? Your quads are screaming. Your feet feel like they are barely leaving the ground. You gasp for breath, even though you're barely moving. In these moments it can be hard to appreciate running. I've had a number of elite runners tell me in interviews over the years that those are the times they remind themselves that they feel lucky to be able to run in the first place—that not everyone has that same opportunity.

What if, even during grueling workouts and lackluster races, we always thought of running as an opportunity, something we *get* to do?

Robert Emmons of University of California, Davis is the foremost expert on gratitude, as well as the editor-in-chief of the *Journal of Positive Psychology*. His research has revealed that keeping a gratitude journal has the power to boost your immune system, reduce aches and pains, lower blood pressure, and enhance sleep. Regardless of where your head is at following a race, your body is in a state of breakdown. In addition to doing things like icing an injury or eating a healthy post-race meal, practicing gratitude can actually influence your recovery. At a lecture of his that I attended at the University of Minnesota, he discussed the ways in which gratitude can heal and energize us both mentally and physically. We become more resilient in the face of adversity and more grateful in the company of joy when we express gratitude. "Gratitude alters our gaze," he said. What's more, it can lead to greater adherence to exercise and also contribute to performance.

Saudi Arabian Olympian Sarah Attar put it to me this way:

> *"I'm often amazed at where running has taken me in life and I am so grateful for these experiences. I think in order to find that calm that one may be seeking, it's important to focus on gratitude. Once a routine of gratitude becomes part of your natural inclination, you find this calm and positive spirit in how you go about everything—especially running. When you're grateful for even just the opportunity and ability to run, it opens up the space within you to become more connected to everything."*

Over time, gratitude becomes an innate skill. As Emmons said in his lecture, "Gratitude is more like an operating system than an app." While you can download a gratitude application on your smartphone and set it to periodically remind you to embrace feelings of well-being and happiness, when a grateful operating system is running in the background at all times, it offers a more constant state of health and wellness.

Exercise 6.5: Take a moment to write down 3–5 things you are grateful for in this moment. While it could have something to do with your running, it could also be related to your family, friends, work, or even the post-race feast you have planned. Try committing to this regularly, once a day or once a week.

Accept Things as They Are

In addition to bolstering your feelings of gratitude, mindfulness trains you not to get so hung up on disappointment—this is how acceptance works. So you had a bad race. While it makes sense to consider how you might modify your execution next time around, rumination is the thief of forward progress. To be sure, this is easier said than done.

The hardest I ever trained for a marathon coalesced on a 90°F (32°C) day at a small-town race in the Midwestern U.S. It was my 13th marathon and the final day to qualify for the following spring's Boston Marathon. All my eggs were in that basket. Despite the high training miles, hard workouts, and extra strength training I put in during the previous four months, I tanked on race day, miscalculating pace and fluid intake in an effort to adjust to the extreme heat and humidity. When I saw my goal time slipping away, I fell apart mentally. Crossing the finish line a good 30 minutes slower than I had hoped, I most certainly muttered a few four-letter words to myself as I stormed away from the finish area past other red-faced, overheated runners sprawled on the grass.

I experienced all manner of negative emotions in the ensuing hours. As we loaded up the car to make the long road trip home, I ran the race in my head again and again. "Where had things gone wrong? What could have I done differently? It's not fair that the weather ended up being so awful! I have the worst luck!" Then I looked over at Jason, who had also run slower than he had hoped, albeit still qualifying for Boston. We had suffered in the heat that day, yet we both finished in one piece. That was a small win in and of itself. Besides, I reminded myself that this was something I got to do, not something I had to do. It suddenly dawned on me that, as Liz Yelling said, "it is just running." I had run plenty of marathons in the past and there'd surely be more in the future.

In fact, just a month later, I did run another marathon. After obsessing about training paces and mileage totals for months and then having a disappointing race, I was burned out when it came to tracking data and striving for any particular time. I decided not to wear a watch—this was a consolation race, so I didn't really care how fast I ran. I just wanted to go out and enjoy it. I was completely surprised when I reached the finish line and saw my time. While it was too late to qualify for Boston that coming spring, I ran fast enough to get in the following year. Letting go of my frustration eliminated pressure and I was able to run my best.

Acceptance simply calls you to say to yourself, "Things didn't go as I had hoped they would, but it doesn't define me as a runner or a person." The mindful philosophy of emphasizing process over results, acknowledgement over denial, and acceptance over judgment offers a different approach to the traditional post-race reflection process. If you're having trouble accepting the outcome of your race, try the following exercise.

Exercise 6.6: Cultivating Acceptance

- Label the feeling that is getting in the way of acceptance. For instance, "I'm feeling really disappointed that I didn't run a personal best today" or "I'm angry that I had to stop and walk mid-way through the race."

- Identify whether the aforementioned emotions are creating tension anywhere in your body. Bring awareness to it and relax if you can.

- Investigate where your emotions are rooted. Are you disappointed because you were hoping to impress your family who supported you during training? Are you angry because you spent a lot of money to sign up for the race only to fall short of your goal?

- Revisit your True North Goal as a way of gaining perspective and reminding yourself that your mindful running practice has greater purpose beyond any single event.

Reflect on Results

While keeping race results in perspective is important, it doesn't mean you can't analyze and learn from your triumphs and mistakes. Applying the skill of fathoming in the context of a post-race reflection can help you apply what you've learned to subsequent performances. Sports psychologist Gloria Petruzzelli recommends doing this a couple days after the race. "Refrain from reflecting on successes and failures until after emotions have subsided," she told me. "This is where the attitudes of nonjudgment, letting go, and self-compassion can be key."

When you do sit down to reflect, it's important to keep in mind that "success" and "failure" are just passing states for the mindful runner. One race performance does not define you as a runner. As Petruzzelli told me, "Mindfulness reminds us that all situations are temporary and therefore we should refrain from attaching too much meaning to them."

Mindfulness can play a key role in helping you put race performances into perspective.

Exercise 6.7: Post-Race Reflection

Grab your training journal and write down the following:

- Three things you felt you did well on race day. This could include things like having a good first mile, remaining positive throughout, or even drinking a little water at every aid station.

- Three things you would like to do differently next time. Maybe your shoe came untied because you didn't tie it tightly enough, you didn't leave enough time to eat breakfast, or you let negative thinking get the better of you in the final mile.

- Two things you would do the same in your training in the future. For instance, maybe you were happy with how many weekly miles you ran or the workouts you did.

- Two things you would change about your training in the future. This might include taking more rest days or starting to train earlier in the season.

Shift Gears

You put in the hard work to train over weeks and months leading up to a big race, eschewing social engagements and putting other projects on the back burner as you prioritized running. You rose early to log miles, ate well, stayed hydrated, and made sure to get enough rest. Life pretty much revolved around your race goal.

Suddenly, a major driving force in your life is gone. Regardless of the race outcome, runners often come down with a nasty case of the post-race blues once the dust settles. "There are neurotransmitters in the brain that aren't balanced out after the exhilarating emotional experience of a race," said Petruzzelli. "This is totally normal and very temporary."

Fortunately, present-moment awareness can help mitigate post-race letdown. As you've probably picked up on in previous chapters, mindfulness emphasizes the impermanence and ever-changing nature of all things. Clinging to your training after your season winds down is a recipe for burnout, but trying to deny feelings of loss following a race isn't the answer either. "It's really important that you just experience those feelings of letdown after a race," coach Lucy Smith emphasized to me. "Getting people just to be aware of the feelings that come up, but not get too attached to them, is the trick."

She has seen athletes more adeptly handle the aftermath of races when they take time to chart out future goals. This allows you to gain perspective and see the bigger picture. "Start planning what the months after the race are going to look like, plan recovery and next season's race calendar," added Smith.

Finally, as you take a little time away from any serious running in order to let your body and mind recover, redirect your attention to other areas of your life that you may have neglected during training. Spend more time with your kids, tackle those home improvement projects, or simply put your feet up and enjoy some down time. Be mindful of the fact that everything you do adds weight to one side of the scale of life and maintaining equilibrium is an important part of the happiness equation.

Chapter 7
BONUS: FUSION

*"It's almost as if I can see more now that I'm blind.
I have to pay closer attention to everything that's
going on around me, so I think I 'see' more of the
world, rather than being oblivious to things. When I'm
running, my mind is totally focused and clear and I just
exist in the moment."*

IMAGINE WAKING UP one morning, opening your eyes and not
being able to see out of your right eye. You blink a few times,
sit up in bed, and try to look around the room. You place your
hand over the right and then the left eye. Nothing but mysterious
flashes of light appear in your right eye, as if you'd been sitting in
a dark room in front of a computer screen for hours. Then, not
long after, the vision in the left eye goes too.

This is what 20-year-old Chaz Davis experienced in early 2013
during his freshman year of college at the University of Hartford
in West Hartford, Connecticut. So began months of tests and
visits to various specialists, most of whom were stumped by his
condition. Finally, about five months after the initial onset, he
got a diagnosis: Leber Hereditary Optic Neuropathy (LHON).
A rare and incurable condition that causes vision loss, this was
particularly shocking considering he had better than normal
vision up until that point.

Secondary to the vision loss, Davis suffered another blow when the initial diagnosing doctor suggested that physical exertion may further damage his eyesight. After winning multiple Massachusetts state titles in high school, he was heavily recruited by college track and cross-country programs. He ended up choosing Hartford, an NCAA Division I program. Not only was he an exceptional athlete, running was his outlet for stress and a defining aspect of his identity. Without his sight and his running, Davis found himself profoundly lost in the world.

"It was devastating," he told me from Denver, Colorado where he studied at the Colorado Center for the Blind. "Running had been my livelihood and when it was taken away, it was a huge setback for me."

Fortunately, a second opinion from another doctor several months later gave him the go-ahead to begin training again. That summer he started by running off the weight he gained during his time away from the sport. In August, he showed up to Hartford's cross-country camp in hopes that he might be able to compete again. "I trained with the team and ran one race, but I fell down numerous times because I wasn't able to navigate the sudden pitch changes on the course," he said. "I felt like I had to attempt it, but it was immediately clear it wasn't going to work out."

He wasn't about to give up that easily, though. Once indoor track season came around, he decided to give that a shot. He figured the predictable footing and the fact that he could very vaguely make out the lane lines might make it feasible. His first race back was the 3,000-meter distance, where he ran far off his personal best. He recalled:

"I was extremely timid in that race and wasn't confident with my foot placement. My focus wasn't in the race as much as on how I was going to navigate the track without

running into someone or running off the track completely.
It was a lot of pressure too because so many people
expected me to make a comeback, so all those worries
were just going through my head at the time."

With each race, though, Davis' confidence grew. He found that when he could let go of his anxieties and expectations and simply concentrate on putting one foot in front of the other, moment-to-moment, things began to click. "I started to focus on just racing, rather than worrying about the potential obstacles I might encounter," he told me. "I felt more like my old self again. It was a huge milestone."

Pretty soon, he discovered that not only was he back to his old self in most respects, he was better than before he lost his vision. Something he had doubted was possible mere months earlier, he began logging performances up to Division I standards again. What's more, not long after his college graduation, he headed to Rio de Janiero to represent the U.S. in the 1,500 meters and 5,000 meters at the 2016 Paralympic Games, where he set personal bests in both distances. He told me:

"When I lost my sight, I thought that life was essentially
over because I couldn't do all the things I once did, but I
pretty quickly figured out that wasn't the case. I just had
to regain my confidence, put the distractions aside and
focus on my path. Now I think life is actually better than
before I lost my vision. I attribute that to running, it really
gave me my life back."

Upon returning home from Rio, Davis continued to run and on just six weeks of marathon-specific training, he debuted in the 26.2-mile distance at the 2016 California International Marathon in Sacramento. Running with a guide, he finished in 2 hours 31 minutes 48 seconds, averaging 5 minutes 47 seconds per mile pace and setting a new American record for a first-time marathoner in the T12/B2 visual impairment category. Had he run that time in the marathon at the Paralympics in Rio, he would have won gold.

Davis says that the experience of losing his vision and finding a new path through running has influenced the way he moves through life in many ways. "I'm not really afraid to do new things now. When I first started getting back into running after losing my sight, I said to myself, 'If you don't try it, you'll never know if you can do it or not. What's the worst that can happen?'" he explained to me. "That's how I approach life now. Things might seem insurmountable and you feel like there's no way you could do something, but you just go and try. I've found putting myself out there is really important."

To be sure, he contends that although he is now blind, he feels like he actually "sees" more than he did before. He told me:

"It's funny because when you're blind, you pay more attention to everything that's going on around you. And when I'm running, I'm so focused, I have this perception that I can see better than I do in my normal life, even though physically that's not the case. I'm just in my element when I'm running. I don't have to use my cane or rely on anyone else or worry about other things, I just feel liberated."

Davis' story is a perfect example of how, when we pay attention, the things we learn from running have a way of enriching our lives far beyond the running trails. Indeed, that's the whole point of integrating the principles of mindfulness into your running routine in the first place. It teaches the mind and body to function in tandem, rather than as two separate systems. You become better at dealing with stress and bouncing back from hardship. Focusing on what's directly in front of you, whether

The lessons learned through mindful running often reach far beyond the trails.

that's work, play, or family, becomes second nature. You even learn to take greater notice of even the smallest joys. By using mindful movement as a training ground for sharpening present-moment awareness, you learn to tune in to life and operate more authentically.

Having spent the past decade listening to and learning from runners from all walks of life, some of the same themes have repeatedly arisen when it comes to what we can gain from embracing running with greater intention. As Davis discovered, harnessing awareness isn't just about seeing what's directly in front of us, but rather, immersing ourselves in the experience body, mind and soul. That's where meaning, purpose, and joy sprout. From the mouths of the experts, the following are some of the most common ways I have learned runners take the lessons gained from their mindful running routines off the trails and into their lives.

Flexibility leads to ease

Sports psychologist Gloria Petruzzelli told me, "The hallmark of a mindful athlete is how well you handle the unexpected."

A story Becky Wade shared with me about her year-long trip running around the globe illustrates this notion: "Running in

Ethiopia was so refreshing because they aren't so reliant on precision. In Western cultures we are taught to care about mileage and exact pace, but there, they don't run with watches and often don't really have a plan regarding how long or fast they are going to go when they head out in a group. It was hard to let go when I was running with them and it put me out of my comfort zone, but it was also really good for me. I've heard the theory that the Ethiopians are so accomplished at cross-country because they are more flexible and adapt more easily when something happens out of their control in a race."

Stress is stress

"I tell the athletes I coach that we all have a stress tolerance level and stress comes from many areas in our lives—work, family running, etc. If stress in one area is too much, it can affect our performances in all areas of our lives. It's all about being aware of these stresses and adapting," Olympian Liz Yelling told me.

"It's important for anyone who is active to put training load in the context of your life," added Eleanor Fish of Run Wild Retreats. "You have to look at your training volume and intensity, but also all the other life stressors that are contributing to your total stress load. Being mindful is vitally important to being able to manage your health and keep things sustainable."

Anxiety doesn't need to rule the day

"A lot of my student athletes say that when they are feeling anxious before an exam, for instance, that they thought about the mindfulness techniques we use during runs and found that it transfers to other situations really well," said coach Steve Magness. "It helps with stress and emotional reactivity so you're no longer a slave to fear and anxiety, which can lead to rumination and an inability to get anything else done."

Thoughts precede action

"If you get wrapped up thinking about yourself and what could go wrong, you're probably going to twist an ankle or fall off a cliff, depending on where you're running," psychiatrist and runner Judson Brewer told me.

Runner and writer Mirna Valerio echoed his point, telling me: "When there are roots and rocks and obstacles, it requires a heightened state of awareness, but not a fear-based awareness, like 'Oh no, I might trip.' I don't know if it's the universe trying to tell me something or if it's just a matter of focus, but when I'm running on trails, the moment I start having negative thoughts about myself, I trip. It never fails. That immediately takes me out of that mindset."

Life is all about perspective

"Being in the back of the pack was never a negative thing for me," said Olympian Sarah Attar, who finished second to last in a time of 3 hours 16 minutes 11 seconds in the marathon at the Rio

Mindful running trains you to live in the moment in all areas of life.

Olympics. "I was so focused on my personal goal and task that it was easy to just run my own race. Rio was very much about embracing the distance and elements."

Curiosity is key

"When you tap into curiosity, that in and of itself feels good and is interesting," explained Brewer. "For instance, you might say to yourself, 'I'm too slow.' When you get curious about that self-judgment, you can identify it as just a thought and figure out what the result of that thought might be. Maybe you'd notice 'Oh, I'm clenching my shoulders.' This is all reward-based learning—when we pay attention, we start to see more clearly the rewards we get or don't get. In that way, our brains recalibrate and start to let go of the self-judgment."

Pain is perceived

Doctor and ultrarunner, Rick Hecht told me: "Mindfulness can help you work with discomfort when you're pushing the limit. The idea coming from much of the recent literature is basically that instead of ignoring and pushing away discomfort, mindfulness leads you to actually pay attention to it in a nonjudgmental way and often you find it doesn't feel as bad as when you're trying to push it away."

Neuroscientist Adrienne Taren added: "This ability to sit with physical discomfort while I'm in the middle of a hard running session—it totally changed how I thought about what my brain is doing when I'm in pain or uncomfortable. It's learning to come outside of your body and observing, 'Okay, this is discomfort I'm feeling because I'm running a hard interval and this feeling is going to be with me the next three minutes and it's probably going to get worse, but that's okay. It doesn't mean I'm going to die.'"

Running connects us

"Paying attention to the terrain, the trees, the others runners on the trail—these are things we might not typically notice or appreciate," said high-performance coach Cindra Kamphoff. "That's the power of a more mindful approach."

Olympian Sarah Attar also told me: "I am so inspired and visually stimulated by the landscapes that I run that I tend to return to those areas to photograph them, which then becomes another form of meditation of the same place in a new way. Running is really such a powerful way to connect with the world around us."

Things are in constant flux

"When we watch the mind, we see how things are always coming and going. If I'm cold or tired at the beginning of a run, I know it's not going to last much beyond that first mile because things are always changing. Or when I wake up in the morning in a bad mood, I know it doesn't mean I'm going to be in a bad mood all day or even an hour later," Terry Pearson, my meditation teacher, told me. "That idea of impermanence can keep us from feeling stuck. Even when you're uncomfortable, you know that moment will pass and things will change."

Suffering can be a catalyst for gratitude

"Even in moments of extreme discomfort in races, I often feel gratitude. I think, 'Wow, this is what it's like to push my limits and I know I'll be stronger and more courageous on the other side.' It's important to count your blessings, even in the hard moments," Olympian Deena Kastor told me, saying that she trained herself to be more grateful over the years by writing in a gratitude journal each night before bed. "Once I got into the habit, I started to look around for things to be grateful for to make my list that night. And when I came across those things again, like an extra-hot cappuccino or the wind blowing through the leaves on the aspen tree outside my house, that moment became more sacred because I had paused to reflect and write it down before."

Happiness is a skill

Meditation researcher Fadel Zeidan told me that people who are trained in mindfulness are often more adept at "experiencing things without placing judgment on them. They are better able to acknowledge and let go."

"You have to create the conditions for happiness," Dr. Roberto Benzo of the Mayo Clinic told me. "You don't find happiness because everything that comes your way is good, it's because you have the flexibility to dance and work with whatever occurs. That creates a sense of balance and contentment, which is where happiness comes from."

Mindful brain training can transform you into a happier and healthier runner and human being.

CHAPTER 8

PUTTING MINDFULNESS INTO PRACTICE

Mindful Running Quick-Start

This quick-start is meant to be used as a crib sheet once you've read and absorbed the *focus-fathom-flow* process. It can also be useful as a reflection activity to help cement the process in your mind. For a more detailed explanation of each step, go back to Chapters 3, 4, and 5.

Step One: Focus

This step is all about simply focusing in and noticing your surroundings, body, and mind as you run.

Environmental Scan

- What do you hear?
- What do you smell?
- What do you taste?
- What do you feel?
- What do you see?

Body Scan

- Bring awareness to the top of your head and forehead.
- Move to your face and jaw.
- Take note of your neck and shoulders.
- Pay attention to your breathing.
- Move to your arms, hands, and fingers.
- Next, scan down your spine to your pelvis.

- Bring awareness to your lower back, abdominals, and hips.
- Travel down the legs, one at a time.
- Finish by placing attention on your feet as they make contact with the ground.

Mental Scan

- What are the top three thoughts running through your mind at the moment?
- What emotions are attached to those thoughts?
- Are the thoughts and emotions affecting you physically?

Step Two: Fathom

This is the action step—where you make necessary adjustments. If you identified any of the following in Step One, these questions will help you determine if you need to do anything about it.

- **Suffering** Are you experiencing the discomfort that accompanies exertion or that of an impending injury? If it's the former, examine it for a moment, label the feelings, and then let them drift on by. Try utilizing your mantra. If it's the latter, slow down or stop running.
- **Fatigue** Is the fatigue related to just being a little worn down or could it be related to overtraining? If it's the former, observe the tiredness, label it and then let it go. Your mantra may again come in handy. If it's the latter, slow down or stop running.
- **Stress** What exactly are you stressing about? Bring awareness to and label the thoughts. Try to let them pass through your mind's sky and allow your body to relax. Work on reframing the anxiety as excitement.
- **Self-Reproach** Ask why you are judging or criticizing yourself? Call out that negative voice. Remind yourself that you are not your thoughts. Before your next run, spend a moment visualizing the runner you want to be.

- **Boredom** Are you bored because of a lack of variety in your training? If so, switch things up by running a new route or workout. If you're simply having trouble with mind wandering, get curious about your stride, breathing, and the way your body is moving through space.
- **Clinging** Are your thoughts tied up in craving or clinging to a particular memory or emotion? Take a moment for gratitude, then let the thoughts pass on through your mind.
- **Brainstorming** Is your mind on overdrive, dreaming up solutions and ideas? Take notice of those thoughts and let them go. Trust that the important thoughts will revisit you at a more opportune time.

Step Three: Flow

If you've engaged in the first two steps, flow will be easier to achieve. This step simply requires you to concentrate on the anchor of your choice.

- Choose an anchor: Breath, feet, or something else that you've found works for you.
- Focus on the in-and-out pattern of your breath or the left-right-left of your feet.
- Get curious about the changing nature of your anchor.
- If you notice your mind wandering, gently bring it back to your anchor and pick up where you left off.

Mindful Yoga

If you're mindfully attending to your health, you probably noticed that relying solely on running for your exercise routine can create both literal and figurative imbalances. Physically, when you perform the same movement over and over, as you do in running, you inevitably neglect certain areas. That's why you might see a talented runner struggle through a strength class at the gym. What's more, taxing the same muscles and pounding the same bones day after day is a recipe for overuse injuries. Similarly, you risk mental burnout if you don't switch up your training routine every now and again. Having another mindful movement practice in your training arsenal will help keep both your body and mind fresh.

Enter mindful yoga. By combining yoga and the principles of mindfulness, you get a low-impact workout in the context of present-moment awareness. It just happens that yoga is a perfect complement to any running routine. Not only can it contribute to better strength, flexibility, and balance, it also can help improve proprioception and kinesthetic awareness.

Additionally, scores of research studies have demonstrated that yoga can enhance cardiovascular function, reduce stress, anxiety, and depression, speed physical recovery, and improve sleep, among other things. What's more, it offers you the chance to deepen your mindfulness practice through a different set of movements.

The following sequence is a basic introduction to mindful yoga. It can be performed in place of a run or in addition to your workout. In a perfect world, you'd do this several times a week to support your mindful running practice and prevent injuries. In the same way that you brought awareness to your body and mind through mindful running, work on staying in the moment as you move through these poses. Any time you find your mind wandering, simply bring it back to your body or breath.

Child's Pose

Start on your hands and knees. Take two deep, slow breaths. Bring your attention to the present moment. As you exhale, bow forward, bringing your torso between your thighs and your forehead to the mat. Extend your arms with palms facing down. Hold and breathe for 60 seconds.

Plank

Get in push-up position, keeping your arms shoulder-width apart and your shoulders stacked in line with your wrists. You should be able to draw a straight line from your heels, to your backside, to your shoulders and head, so be careful not to let your midsection dip. Engage your entire core to maintain the position. Breathe, and hold for 30–60 seconds.

Upward Facing Dog

Go directly from Plank to Cobra by bending your elbows and lowering your body down to the mat like you would when doing a push-up, being careful to squeeze your elbow in towards your ribcage rather than flaring them out. Shift your foot position by pressing the tops of your feet into the mat. Then on the inhale, carefully straighten your arms, stacking your shoulders directly over your wrists and lifting your chest. At this point, if you are feeling strong, you can proceed from the Cobra position into Upward Dog by fully lifting your pelvis and thighs off the mat. Hold the pose for 10 seconds, breathing in and out.

Downward Facing Dog

Transition from Upward Facing Dog by bringing your body back into Plank position. In a fluid motion, exhale as you push your thighs back, reach your pelvis toward the sky, and bring your heels to the mat. Straighten your legs, but be careful not to lock your knees. Envision your hips and thighs being pulled back as you press your palms into the floor and lift your pelvis. Hold for 10–20 seconds as you breathe.

High Crescent Lunge

From Down Dog, inhale as you raise your right leg straight into the air ("Three-Legged Dog"). Then, as you exhale, draw in and up through your core and shift your body forward as you bend your right knee and bring it under your body. Plant it between your hands on the mat. Inhale as you raise your chest to an upright position and draw your arms up overhead. Your palms should be open and facing one another and your gaze directed slightly upward. Hold for 20–30 seconds as you breathe in and out. Then, step back to the mat in Down Dog and come up into lunge position on the other side.

Forward Fold

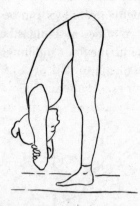

From High Crescent Lunge, step up and stand with your feet together, back straight, and arms at your side ("Mountain Pose"). Breathe in and out. Soften your knees and exhale as you fold your torso down over your legs. Place your hands next to your feet or let them hang. Hold for 30–60 seconds as you breathe.

Cat/Cow

Come down to your hands and knees on the mat and align your shoulders with your wrists and your hips with your knees. Exhale as you draw your belly toward your spine, rounding your back and bringing your head toward the floor ("Cat pose"). Then inhale and move your belly toward the mat as you bring your chest forward and your gaze to the sky ("Cow pose"). Repeat this sequence 5–10 times as you slowly breathe in and out.

Happy Baby

Lie on your back on the mat. Exhale as you bring your knees toward your belly. Grip your feet with your hands. Gently rock back and forth for 20–30 seconds as you breathe.

Savasana

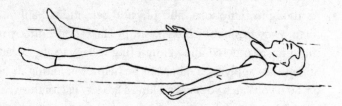

Also called "Corpse pose," Savasana simply calls you to relax on your back with your arms and legs outstretched. The key is to allow your body to completely let go as you simply exist with your breath.

Basic Seated Mindfulness Meditation

As has been discussed, seated meditation isn't for everyone. I certainly never expected to buy in, but after garnering so many benefits from my mindful running practice, I became convinced to try it. I've found that it is a great tool to have available when I'm feeling stressed or anxious, but I can't go for a run. You can meditate just about anywhere—on the train on the way to work, while you brush your teeth or as I sometimes do, while rocking my baby girl to sleep. It can be a quick moment of focusing on your breath or your baby's breath and calming your mind or a more formal seated meditation for five minutes or beyond. Here are the basic instructions for a seated session:

- Find a place to sit comfortably upright with good, relaxed posture. If you can stay awake, you can also lie down in Savasana if you prefer.
- Focus in on your breath. Choose to direct your attention to the nostrils, chest or belly as you breathe, wherever your respiration feels most prominent. Follow each breath from its start to its end, getting curious about how it changes with each inhale and exhale. Really work on feeling the air moving in and out of your body.
- As thoughts, emotions, and physical sensations haul your focus away from your breath, simply take notice that your mind has wandered and gently bring it back to the breath. Sometimes applying a label can be helpful in letting things go. So if you catch yourself making a grocery list for the week, label it "planning," or if you find you're getting carried away thinking about the ache in your shoulder, label it "tension." Then just bring your awareness back to your breath, again and again every time your mind wanders.

Basic Walking Mindfulness Meditation

If you're having trouble dialing in to your running workouts with full attention, you may need to walk before you can run. Walking meditation is a key part of Mindfulness-Based Stress Reduction training, offering yet another way to tap into your body and mind. You can do this just about anywhere—pacing back and forth in your living room, walking in the woods, or even hoofing it down a city street on your way to work. Here are basic instructions for walking meditation:

- Stand with your feet shoulder-width apart and bring awareness to your surroundings, body, and mind. Become aware of any physical sensations and take a couple of deep belly breaths.
- Slowly step forward with your right foot, paying attention to lifting the foot, swinging it forward, placing it back on the ground in front of your body, and transferring your weight to that side.
- Then do the same with the left foot.
- Imagine yourself in slow motion as you become aware of when you lift, swing, and plant.
- Really tune in to each distinct movement that makes up the gait cycle.
- Bring attention to the bottom of your feet with each step as they make contact with the ground.
- Continue breathing deeply as your body relaxes.

Mindful Brick Workout

As was demonstrated in the studies on "MAP Training" (Mental and Physical) conducted by neuroscientists at Rutgers University that I mentioned in Chapter 1, combining conventional seated meditation and running can pack a powerful punch. To do this, follow the aforementioned 10-minute basic seated meditation, then lace up and head out for a run. Take note of how this changes your experience. I often do this and find it can transform a run from two-dimensions to high definition.

Mindfulness Hacks

Mindful Moments

Even if you want to try conventional meditation, many of us just flat-out don't have the time. That's why I like an idea that the *New York Times* best-selling author and famed meditation teacher Sharon Salzberg often refers to as "short moments, many times." This serves as a perfect on-ramp for bringing mindfulness into your everyday life.

All it requires is putting down your smartphone and backing away from your computer for 30–60 seconds, breathing deeply, and dialing in to the present. I often practice this for a moment while waiting for my coffee to brew in the morning or as I empty the dishwasher. It helps me recognize how hurried and amped up I get without noticing. A few simple breaths take me from frazzled to calm in no time.

Seeing Blue

We often don't even realize how much of our experiences we miss because we are so lost in thought. All you have to do for this exercise is choose a color and commit to noticing every variation of it on a particular day. I like using the color blue because, other than the sky, it doesn't appear as often in the natural world as brown or green, for instance. When I come across it, it really stands out.

For instance, on my first day-long silent meditation retreat, instead of taking an hour for lunch in the middle of the day, I decided to lace up and run the marshy trails behind the fitness center where the retreat was being held. Having meditated all morning, I easily slipped into a focused and relaxed mindset as I watched my breath hit the cold air with each exhale as I ran.

When I reached the furthest point away from the fitness center on the looped trail, I stopped and looked out over the marsh. The sky was gray, there were no leaves on the trees, and the brittle, dried cattails of the marsh were still partially buried by snow and ice. Off in the distance, though, a blue silo-shaped building popped right out of the landscape. It struck me how vivid it was against the monochromatic scene—like a color accent in a black and white photograph. Later, I realized, fittingly, that the blue structure was the fitness center's meditation tower.

As you begin purposely looking for a certain color in your day, you'll likely have a similar experience where you discover that simply being more aware serves to make the way you see the world more vibrant and dynamic. Seeing blue (or any color) just highlights that experience.

Mindful Memo

If you're anything like me, you'll find that bringing mindfulness to the run is often easier than achieving it in everyday life. As such, when I'm stressed or in the midst of a busy week, I leave myself what I call "mindful memos" in key places. Usually this is just a little piece of paper that says "breathe," which I stick on the bathroom mirror or above the sink in the kitchen. While this sounds a little hokey, it works surprisingly well to snap me out of my mind's tendency to run at a million miles per hour. When I notice the memo, I take two deep and very mindful breaths before proceeding with my day.

Jitter Jar

This is a great visualization aid prior to competition to combat pre-race jitters. It's also a fun project to do with your kids. Basically, this is a jar full of water, glitter, and a little glue that represents your mind when you're feeling stressed. Shake the jar and the glitter (your thoughts, feelings and emotions) go swirling. This prevents you from being able to see through the jar—similar to how you can't think clearly when you're stressed. When you wait for the glitter to settle, your thoughts, feelings and emotions do the same, thereby allowing you to make better decisions. For a more in-depth explanation, flip back to Chapter 3. Here's how to make your very own Jitter Jar:

Supplies:

- Glass mason jar or clear plastic bottle
- Glitter glue or clear gel glue
- 3–5 teaspoons of fine glitter (depending on the size of the jar)
- 1 drop of food coloring, the same color as the glitter
- Enough hot water to fill ¾ of your jar

1. Mix the hot water and glue. Depending on how slowly you want your glitter to swirl before settling, you can add more or less glue.
2. Drop in the glitter and food coloring.
3. Put the top on and glue it shut.

Gratitude Bottle

Have you ever thought, "I wish I could just bottle so-and-so's attitude!" Well, here's your chance. A Gratitude Bottle can be any old water bottle you have sitting around. A few times a week, after a run, write something down that you noticed on the run and feel grateful for. This could be anything from "I'm grateful that my legs felt fresh today" or "I'm grateful to live in a place that has so many beautiful places to run" or "I'm grateful I hit my goal pace today." Then fold up that piece of paper and stick it in the bottle. On days you're feeling less than enthusiastic about running, all you have to do is hit the bottle, so to speak. With time, you might find that you naturally tune in and become more appreciative on runs because you're looking for things to add to the bottle.

A wholehearted pursuit of your True North via mindful running sets the stage for a richer experience on the trails and beyond.

ACKNOWLEDGEMENTS

A book about mindfulness wouldn't be complete without some words of gratitude. My deepest thanks to all the runners who shared their stories with me. I never cease to be amazed by how this simple act of movement can change lives. Thank you to all the brilliant minds in the fields of neuroscience, psychology, meditation, and exercise science who were willing to share their knowledge and expertise with me. A special thanks goes to my MBSR teacher, Terry Pearson, and a long list of others who influenced my thinking about mindfulness.

This book wouldn't have happened without my excellent and patient editor at Bloomsbury, Matthew Lowing. He was willing to take a chance on me and give me the freedom to tackle this project as I saw fit. His editorial guidance has been invaluable.

Huge gratitude goes to my willing first readers: Jason Havey, Ted Lobby, Sam Lobby, Ann Havey, Amanda Jeske, and Alison Sipkins. Your feedback and ideas make me feel fortunate to have such smart folks in my inner circle.

I've discovered along the way that it truly takes a village to raise a child, especially when you're also writing a book. My deepest heartfelt thanks go to our amazing support system, who have shown so much love to our newborn baby girl and us. Chief among them are my dad, a top-notch grandpa and the person who taught me to love to run. Thanks also to my brother, who is always a willing shoulder to lean on. We couldn't have done it without my wonderful in-laws, Ann and John Havey. To the Prebils, the Massopusts, the Jeskes, the McPheeters, and the entire Abbott Crew, I'll never be able to repay your kindness.

To my husband, Jason, words cannot adequately express the deep gratitude I feel for you. You are the love of my life, my best friend, running partner, and greatest support. I am indebted to our always-enthusiastic vizsla pup, Welly, for getting me out the door to run on even the most brutally cold days in January and slowest days of pregnancy. And of course, to my spunky baby girl, Liesl—you keep me on my toes and running every single day. How I got so lucky to be your mama, I don't know. I love you three to the moon and back.

ABOUT THE AUTHOR

Mackenzie L. Havey (née Lobby) writes about endurance sports, mind/body health and wellness and adventure travel. Her work has appeared in *Runner's World*, *SELF*, *Triathlete*, *TheAtlantic.com*, *ESPN.com*, *OutsideOnline.com* and elsewhere. In addition to completing 14 marathons and an Ironman triathlon, she is a USA Track & Field-certified coach, an instructor in the Physical Activity Program in the School of Kinesiology at the University of Minnesota and has done training in Mindfulness-Based Stress Reduction. She studied English at the College of St. Benedict and has a master's in kinesiology with an emphasis in sport and exercise psychology from the University of Minnesota. She lives with her husband, daughter, and vizsla in Minneapolis.

MindfulRunningBook.com

MLHavey.com

RESOURCES

Preface

A buzzing throng … New York Road Runners (2014), 'Record-breaking numbers at the 44th running of the TCS New York City Marathon'. <http://www.nyrr.org/media-center/press-releases/record-breaking-numbers-at-the-44th-running-of-the-tcs-new-york-city-marathon> [Accessed March 2017]

To all the runners … Ngo, E., Lauterbach, J., Alvarez, M., Pereira, I., Montero, N., and Ferney, S.A. (2014), 'New York marathon competitors challenged by cold, wind'. <http://www.newsday.com/news/new-york/wilson-kipsang-mary-keitany-kenyans-win-2014-new-york-city-marathon-in-windy-cold-conditions-1.9566397> [Accessed March 2017]

The contrast was … Wittenberg, M. Author interview 2 March 2017.

When the flakes settle … Pearson, T. Author interview 30 March 2017.

Introduction

Running is meditation … Kastor, D. Author interview 4 April 2017.

You don't even want … Kastor, D. Author interview 4 April 2017.

You're already … Brewer, J. (2013), 'You're already awesome. Just get out of your own way!' <https://www.youtube.com/watch?v=jE1j5Om7g0U> [Accessed December 2016]

Most people live … James, W. (1902), *The Varieties of Religious Experience*, Edinburgh: University of Edinburgh. <http://www.giffordlectures.org/lectures/varieties-religious-experience> [Accessed January 2017]

epidemic of hurrying … Popova, M. (2016), 'Sam Harris on the paradox of meditation and how to stretch our capacity for everyday self-transcendence'. <https://www.brainpickings.org/2014/09/29/sam-harris-waking-up-meditation/> [Accessed March 2017]

Stories abound … Pedersen, N. (2011), 'The Lung-Gom-Pa Runners of Old Tibet', *Trail Runner Magazine*.

strange traveler … David-Neel, A. (1971), *Magic and Mystery in Tibet*, New York: Dover.

Marathon monks … Finn, A. (2015), 'What I learned when I met the monk who ran 1,000 marathons'. <https://www.theguardian.com/lifeandstyle/2015/mar/31/japanese-monks-mount-hiei-1000-marathons-1000-days> [Accessed February 2017]

Running offers athletes … Magness, S. Author interview 19 March 2017.

It's about simply … Brewer, J. Author interview 16 March 2017.

The value of … Sherlin, L. Author interview 9 March 2017.

Hoping for a new … Sheehan, G. (2014) *Running and being: The Total Experience*, Pennsylvania: Rodale.

Long distance running ... Shainberg, D. (1977), 'Long distance running as meditation'. *Annals of the New York Academy of Sciences,* 301: 1002–1009.

Chapter 1

I focused on ... Olson, T. (2012), 'Life to the Utmost'. <http://www.irunfar. com/2012/07/laughing-out-loud-timothy-olsons-2012-western-states-100-race-report.html> [Accessed January 2017]

The footpath was ... 'Western States 100-Mile Endurance Run'. <http://www.wser. org/> [Accessed February 2017]

Bad choices ... Olson, T. (2012), 'My Path to Contentment: From addict to awakened ultrarunner'. <http://www.irunfar.com/2012/04/my-path-to-contentment-from-addict-to-awakened-ultrarunner.html> [Accessed February 2017]

I noticed the ... Olson, T. Author interview 25 August 2016 and 28 February 2017.

Neuroplasticity ... Merzenich, M. (2017), 'On the brain'. <http://www.onthebrain. com/brain-plasticity/> [Accessed December 2016]

Neuroplasticity is the brain's ... Zeidan, F. Author interview 9 March 2017.

virtuoso violinists ... Jancke, L. (2009), 'Music drives brain plasticity'. *F1000 Biology Reports,* 1:78.

jugglers ... Draganski, B., Gaser, C., Volker, B. Schuierer, G., Bogdahn, U. and May, A. (2004), 'Neuroplasticity: Changes in grey matter induced by training'. *Nature,* 427: 311–312.

taxi drivers ... Maguire, E.A., Woollett, K. and Spiers, H.J. (2006), 'London taxi drivers and bus drivers: a structural MRI and neuropsychological analysis'. *Hippocampus,* 16(12): 1091–1101.

Researchers at the ... Azevedo, F.A., Carvalho, L.R.B., Grinberg, L.T., Farfel, J.M., Ferretti, R.E.L., Leite, R.E.P., Filho, W.J., Lent, R. and Herculano-Houzel, S. (2009), 'Equal numbers of neuronal and nonneuronal cells make the human brain an isometrically scaled-up primate brain'. *The Journal of Comparative Neurology,* 513(5): 532–541.

neurons that fire ... Hebb, D.O. (1949), *The Organization of Behavior,* New York: Wiley.

Over time and ... Mooney, R.A., Coxon, J.P., Cirillo, J., Glenny, H., Gant, N. and Byblow, W.D. (2016), 'Acute aerobic exercise modulates primary motor cortex inhibition'. *Experimental Brain Research,* 234(12): 3669–3676.

scores of studies ... Nokia, M., Lensu, S., Ahtiainen, J.P., Johansson, P.P., Koch, L.G., Britton, S.L. and Kainulainen, H. (2016), 'Physical exercise increases adult hippocampal neurogenesis in male rats provided it is aerobic and sustained'. *The Journal of Physiology,* 594(7): 1855–1873.

scores of studies ... Schmolesky, M.T., Webb, D.L. and Hansen, R.A. (2013), 'The effects of aerobic exercise intensity and duration on levels of brain-derived neurotrophic factor in healthy men'. *Journal of Sports Science and Medicine,* 12(3): 502–511.

scores of studies ... Cho, S.Y. & Roh, H.T. (2016), 'Effects of aerobic exercise training on peripheral brain-derived neurotrophic factor and eotaxin-1 levels in obese young men'. *Journal of Physical Therapy Science,* 28(4): 1355–1358.

stressful life experiences ... Veena, J., Shankaranarayana Rao, B.S. and Srikumar, B.N. (2011), 'Regulation of adult neurogenesis in the hippocampus by stress, acetylcholine and dopamine'. *Journal of Natural Science, Biology and Medicine*, 2(1): 26–37.

stressful life experiences ... Mirescu, C. and Gould, E. (2006), 'Stress and adult neurogenesis'. *Hippocampus*, 16(3): 233–238.

There will be ... Thoreau, H.D. (2012), *The Portable Thoreau*, New York: Penguin Classics.

which is thought to occur ... Shaffer, J. (2016), 'Neuroplasticity and Clinical Practice: Building Brain Power for Health'. *Frontiers in Psychology*, 7: 1118.

This contributes to ... Erickson, K.I., Leckie, R.L. and Weinstein, A.M. (2014), 'Physical activity, fitness, and gray matter volume'. *Neurobiology of Aging*, 35(2): S20–S28.

brain-boosting ... Hölzel, B.K., Carmody, C., Vangel, M., Congleton, C., Yerramsetti, S.M., Gard, T. and Lazar, S.W. (2011), 'Mindfulness practice leads to increases in regional brain gray matter density'. *Psychiatry Research*, 191(1): 36–43.

stress, anxiety and depression ... Goyal, M., Singh, S., Sibinga, E.M., Gould, N.F., Rowland-Seymour, A., Sharma, R., Berger, Z., Sleicher, D., Maron, D.D., Shihab, H.M., Ranasinghe, P.D., Linn, S., Saha, S., Bass, E.B., Haythornthwaite, J.A. (2014), 'Meditation programs for psychological stress and well-being: a systematic meta-analysis'. *JAMA Internal Medicine*, 174(3): 357–368.

reduce markers of inflammation ... Demarzo, M.M., Montero-Marin, J., Cuijpers, P., Zabaleta-del-Olmo, E., Mahtani, K.R., Vellinga, A., Vicens, C., López-del-Hoyo, Y., Garcia-Campayo, J. (2015), 'The efficacy of mindfulness-based interventions in primary care: A meta-analytic review'. *Annals of Family Medicine*, 13(6): 573–582.

fortify the immune system ... Black, D.S. and Slavich, G.M. (2016), 'Mindfulness meditation and the immune system: a systematic review of randomized controlled trials'. *Annals of The New York Academy of Sciences*, 1373: 13–24.

lowered blood pressure ... Barnes, V.A., Pendergrast, R.A., Harshfield, G.A. and Treiber, F.A. (2008), 'Impact of breathing awareness meditation on ambulatory blood pressure and sodium handling in prehypertensive African American adolescents'. *Ethnicity and Disease*, 18(1): 1–5.

improvements in sleep ... Ong, J.C., Shapiro, S.L. and Manber, R. (2008), 'Combining mindfulness meditation with cognitive-behavior therapy for insomnia: A treatment-development study'. *Behavior Therapy*, 39(2): 171–182.

overall quality of life ... Reibel, D.K., Greeson, J.M., Brainard, G.C. & Rosenzweig, S. (2001), 'Mindfulness-based stress reduction and health-related quality of life in a heterogenous patient population'. *General Hospital Psychiatry*, 23: 183–192.

overall quality of life ... Carlson, L.E., Speca, M., Patel, K.D. & Goodey, E. (2004), 'Mindfulness-based stress reduction in relation to quality of life, mood, symptoms of stress and levels of cortisol, dehydroepiandrosterone sulfate (DHEAS) and melatonin in breast and prostate cancer outpatients'. *Psychoneuroendocrinology*, 29(4): 448–474.

architecture of the ... Lazar, S.W., Kerr, C.E., Wasserman, R.H., Gray, J.R., Greve, D.N., Treadway, M.T., McGarvey, M., Quinn, B.T., Dusek, J.A., Benson, H., Rauch, S.L., Moore, C.I. and Fischl, B. (2005), 'Meditation experience is associated with increased cortical thickness'. *Neuroreport*, 16(17): 1893–1897.

research conducted by … Brewer, J.A., Worhunsky, P.D., Gray, J.R., Tang, Y.Y., Weber, J. and Kober, H. (2011), 'Meditation experience is associated with differences in default mode network activity and connectivity'. *Proceedings of the National Academy of Sciences,* 108(50): 20254–20259.

from contemplative neuroscience … Lutz, A., Brefczynski-Lewis, J., Johnstone, T. and Davidson, R.J. (2008), 'Regulation of the neural circuitry of emotion by compassion meditation: effects of meditative expertise'. *PLOS One,* 3(3): e1897.

Further meditation research … Davidson, R.J. and Begley, S. (2012), *The Emotional Life of Your Brain: How its patterns affect the way you think, feel and live—and How You Can Change Them,* London: Penguin.

This suggests that … Bajaj, B. and Pande, N. (2016), 'Mediating role of resilience in the impact of mindfulness on life satisfaction and affect as indices of subjective well-being'. *Personality and Individual Differences,* 93: 63–67.

The thinking goes … Davidson, R.J. and Lutz, A. (2008), 'Buddha's Brain: Neuroplasticity and Meditation'. *IEEE Signal Processing Magazine,* 25(1): 176–174.

Mindfulness gives you … Taren, A. Author interview 15 March 2017.

Mindfulness meditation trains … Zeidan, F. Author interview 15 March 2017.

Mindfulness and running … Sherlin, L. Author interview 9 March 2017.

weeks of genesis … Anderson, M.L., Sisti, H.M., Curlik, D.M. and Shors, T.J. (2011), 'Associative learning increases adult neurogenesis during a critical period'. *European Journal of Neuroscience,* 33(1): 175–181.

While they don't yet … Shors, T.J., Anderson, L.M., Curlik, D.M. and Nokia, S.M. (2012), 'Use it or lose it: How neurogenesis keeps the brain fit for learning'. *Behavioural Brain Research,* 227(2): 450–458.

I was chatting … Shors, T. Author interview 9 March 2017.

MAP training … Shors, T.J., Olson, R.L., Bates, M.E., Selby, E.A. and Alderman, B.L. (2014), 'Mental and Physical (MAP) Training: A neurogenesis-inspired intervention that enhances health in humans'. *Neurobiology of Learning and Memory,* 115: 3–9.

MAP training … Alderman, B.L., Olson, R.L., Brush, C.J. and Shors, T.J. (2016), 'MAP training: combining meditation and aerobic exercise reduces depression and rumination while enhancing synchronized brain activity'. *Translational Psychiatry,* 6(2): 726.

I'm always looking … Valerio, M. Author Interview 14 March 2017.

Then in 2010 … Killingsworth, M.A. and Gilbert, D.T. (2010), 'A wandering mind is an unhappy mind'. *Science,* 330 (6006): 932.

One 2015 study by Dutch … Tsafou, K.E., De Ridder, D.T., van Ee, R. and Lacroix, J.P. (2016), 'Mindfulness and satisfaction in physical activity: A cross-sectional study in the Dutch population'. *Journal of Health Psychology,* 21(9): 1817–27.

Mindfulness helps me … Hecht, R. Author interview 15 March 2017.

I consciously shifted … Pappas, A. (2016) 'My Pal, Pain'. <http://www.lennyletter. com/life/a510/my-pal-pain/> [Accessed February 2017]

Tracktown … Pappas, A. (2016) 'Tracktown'. <http://tracktownmovie.com/> [Accessed January 2017]

During races … Pappas, A. (2017) Author interview 20 February and 16 March 2017.

psychological skills training … Rothlin, P., Birrer, D., Horvath, S. and Grosse Holtforth, M. (2016), 'Psychological skills training and a mindfulness-based intervention to enhance functional athletic performance: design of a randomized controlled trial using ambulatory assessment'. *BMC Psychology*, 4: 39.

Ironic process theory … Wegner, D.M. (1994), 'Ironic processes of mental control'. *Psychological Review*, 101(1): 34–52.

Try to pose … Dostoevsky, F. (1863), *Winter Notes on Summer Impressions*, Evanston, IL: Northwestern University Press.

There are all … Taren, A. Author interview 15 March 2017.

As psychologist Susan David … David, S. (2016) *Emotional Agility: Get Unstuck, Embrace Change, and Thrive in Work and Life*, New York: Penguin Random House

Researchers at the … Thompson, R.W., Kaufman, K.A., De Petrillo, L.A., Glass, C.R. and Arnkoff, D.B. (2011), 'One year follow-up of Mindful Sport Performance Enhancement (MPSE) With archers, golfers, and runners'. *Journal of Clinical Sport Psychology*, 5: 99–116.

In learning to accept … Bernier, M., Thienot, E., Codron, R. and Fournier, J.F. (2009), 'Mindfulness and acceptance approaches in sport performance'. *Journal of Clinical Sport Psychology*, 3(4): 320–333.

helps an athlete … Sherlin, L. Author interview 9 March 2017.

Research even suggests that … Stevinson, C.D. and Biddle, S.J. (1998), 'Cognitive orientations in marathon running and "hitting the wall"'. *British Journal of Sports Medicine*, 32 (3): 229–235.

Some experts believe … De Petrillo, L.A., Kaufman, K.A., Glass, C.R. and Arnkoff, D.B. (2009), 'Mindfulness for long-distance runners: an open trial using mindful sport performance enhancement (MSPE)'. *Journal of Clinical Sports Psychology*, 4: 357–376.

Chapter 2

If you had told me … Falbo, T. Author interview 21 June 2016.

At that point I … Havey, M.L., 'How running changed these four people's lives'. *Competitor*, 13 September 2016.

upwards of 50 percent … Wilson, K. and Brookfield, D. (2011), 'Effect of goal setting on motivation and adherence in a six-week exercise program'. *International Journal of Sport and Exercise Psychology*, 7(1): 89–100.

it takes an average … Lally, P., Van Jaarsveld, C.H., Potts, H.W. and Wardle, J. (2010), 'How are habits formed: Modelling habit formation in the real world'. *European Journal of Social Psychology*, 40(6): 998–1009.

decision fatigue … Vohs, K.D., Baumeister, R.F., Schmeichel, B.J., Twenge, J.M., Nelson, N.M. and Tice, D.M. (2008, 'Making choices impairs subsequent self control: A limited-resource account of decision making, self-regulation, and active initiative'. *Journal of Personality and Social Psychology*, 94(5): 883–898.

growth mindset … Dweck, C.S. (2006), *Mindset: The New Psychology of Success*, New York: Penguin Random House.

A growth mindset indicates that … Petruzzelli, G. Author interview 26 March 2017.

Trigger. Behavior. Reward … Brewer, J. (2017), *The Craving Mind: From cigarettes to smartphones to love—why we get hooked and how we can break bad habits,* New Haven, Connecticut: Yale University Press.

eating a cupcake … Brewer, J. Author interview 16 March 2017.

The real voyage … Proust, M. (1982), *Remembrance of Things Past,* New York: Vintage.

Each day the run … Shainberg, D. (1977), 'Long distance running as meditation'. *Annals of the New York Academy of Sciences,* 301: 1002–1009.

a 2016 study by French … Ruffault, A., Bernier, M., Juge, N. and Fournier, J.F. (2016), 'Mindfulness may moderate the relationship between intrinsic motivation and physical activity: a cross-sectional study'. *Mindfulness,* 7(2): 445–452.

When you get a … Lobby, M. (2012), 'The Bliss List'. *Runner's World Magazine.*

people who report being mindful … Tsafou, K.E., De Ridder, D.T., van Ee, R. and Lacroix, J.P. (2016), 'Mindfulness and satisfaction in physical activity: a cross-sectional study in the Dutch population'. *Journal of Health Psychology,* 21(9): 1817–1827.

harmonious passion … Vallerand, R.J. (2012), 'The role of passion in sustainable psychological well-being'. *Psychology of Well-Being,* 2: 1.

We are what we … Durant, W. (1991), *The Story of Philosophy: The lives and opinions of the world's greatest philosophers,* New York: Pocket Books.

As a recent Harvard Business School … Ordóñez, L.D., Schweitzer, M.E., Galinsky, A.D. and Bazerman, M.H. (2009), 'Goals Gone Wild: The systematic side effects of over-prescribing goal setting'. *Harvard Business School Review.*

What mindfulness teaches … Fish, E. Author interview 4 March 2017.

I never jump … Lecomte, B. (2015), 'Ben Lecomte swam across the Atlantic; next he tries the Pacific'. <http://www.npr.org/2015/08/23/433926565/ben-lecomte-swam-across-the-atlantic-next-he-tries-the-pacific> [Accessed January 2017]

Your core values … David, S. (2016), *Emotional Agility: Get unstuck, embrace change, and thrive in work and life,* New York: Penguin Random House.

Utah-based runner … Havey, M.L. (2016), 'How running changed these four people's lives', *Competitor,* 13 September 2016.

S.M.A.R.T. Goals … Doran, G. T. (1981), 'There's a S.M.A.R.T. way to write management's goals and objectives'. *Management Review,* 70(11): 35–36.

Outside in nature … Qing, L. (2010), 'Effect of forest bathing trips on human immune function'. *Environmental Health and Preventive Medicine,* 15(1): 9–17.

Chapter 3

Being present while running … Attar, S. Author interview 28 February 2017.

My personal rhythm … Attar, S. Author interview 28 February 2017.

Each day I discover … Sheehan, G. (1978), *Running & Being,* New York: Rodale.

there's something about aerobic … Schmidt-Kassow, M., Deusser, M., Thiel, C., Otterbein, S., Montag, C., Reuter, M., Banzer, W. and Kaiser, J. (2013), 'Physical exercise during encoding improves vocabulary learning in young adult females: a neuroendrocrinological study'. *PLOS One*, 8(5).

Whether it's mulling … Chapman, S.B., Aslan, S., Spence, J.S., Defina, L.F., Keebler, M.W., Didehbani, N. and Lu, H. (2013), 'Shorter term aerobic exercise improves brain, cognition, and cardiovascular fitness in aging'. *Frontiers in Aging Neuroscience*, 5:75.

Run the World … Wade, B. (2016), *Run the World: My 3,500-mile journey through running cultures around the globe*, New York: HarperCollins.

Running definitely serves … Wade, B. Author interview 14 March, 2017.

Let your senses rip … Brewer, J. (2017), *10% Happier Podcast*. #61.

I was at my lowest … Fish, E. Author interview 4 March 2017.

Run Wild Retreats … Fish, E. (2010), 'Run Wild Retreats + Wellness'. <http://runwildretreats.com/> [Accessed December 2016]

According to fossil evidence … Bramble, D.M. and Lieberman, D.E. (2004), 'Endurance running and the evolution of *homo*'. *Nature*, 432: 345–352.

the numbers vary … Davis, I.S., Bowser, B.J. and Mullineaux, D.R. (2016), 'Greater vertical impact loading in female runners with medically diagnosed injuries: a prospective investigation'. *British Journal of Sports Medicine*, 50(14): 887–892.

37 percent … Van Mechelen, W. (1992), 'Running injuries. A review of the epidemiological literature'. *Sports Medicine*, 14(5): 320–335.

79 percent … Van Gent, R.N., Siem, D., Van Middelkoop, M., Van Os, A.G., Bierma-Zeinstra, S.M. and Koes, B.W. (2007), 'Incidence and determinants of lower extremity running injuries in long distance runners: a systematic review'. *British Journal of Sports Medicine*. 41(8): 469–480.

His 2009 study … Lieberman, D.E., Venkadesan, M., Werbel, W.A., Daoud, A.I., D'Andrea, S., Davis, I.S., Mang'Eni, R.O., Pitsiladis, Y. (2010), 'Foot strike patterns and collision forces in habitually barefoot versus shod runners'. *Nature*, 463: 531–535.

Christopher McDougall's international … McDougall, C. (2011), *Born to Run: A hidden tribe, superathletes, and the greatest race the world has never seen*, New York: Vintage.

My research and … Lobby, M. (2011), 'Footstrike, Not Footwear'. *Running Times*.

Case in point … Larson, P. (2010), 'Elite men in the 2010 Boston Marathon—Super slow motion'. <https://vimeo.com/11574503> [accessed November 2016]

what 94 percent … Kasmer, M.E., Liu, X.C., Roberts, K.G. and Valadao, J.M. (2013), 'Foot-strike pattern and performance in a marathon'. *International Journal of Sports Physiology and Performance*, 8(3): 286–292.

hard on your knees … Landreneau, L.L., Watts, K., Heitzman, J.E. and Childers, W.L. (2014), 'Lower limb muscle activity during forefoot and rearfoot strike running techniques'. *International Journal of Sports Physical Therapy*, 9(7): 888–897.

Contrary to a common … Waitz, G. (2010), *Run Your First Marathon: Everything you need to know to reach the finish line*, New York: Skyhorse Publishing.

Anywhere from 18,000 … 'Your nose, the guardian of your lungs'. <http://www.entnet.org/content/your-nose-guardian-your-lungs> [accessed March 2017]

A recent study by anthropology … Zaidi, A.A., Mattern, B.C., Claes, P., McEcoy, B., Hughes, C. and Shriver, M.D. (2017), 'Investigating the case of human nose shape and climate adaptation'. *PLOS Genetics.*

Entrainment of locomotion … Daley, M.A., Bramble, D.M. and Carrier, D.R. (2013), 'Impact loading and locomotor-respiratory coordination significantly influence breathing dynamics in running humans'. *PLOS One,* 8(8): e70752.

Famed running coach … Daniels, J. (2014), *Daniels' Running Formula,* Illinois: Human Kinetics.

runners are successful anywhere … Bramble, D.M. and Carrier, D.R. (1983), 'Running and breathing in mammals'. *Science,* 219(4582): 251–256.

Rhythmic breathing … Daley, M.A., Bramble, D.M. and Carrier, D.R. (2013), 'Impact loading and locomotor-respiratory coordination significantly influence breathing dynamics in running humans'. *PLOS One,* 8(8): e70752.

When a group of researchers … Radomsky, A.S., Alcolado, G.M., Abramowitz, J.S., Alonso, P., Bellock, A., Bouvard, M., Clark, D.A., Coles, M.E., Doron, G., Fernández-Álvarez, H., Garcia-Soriano, G., Ghisi, M., Gomez, B., Inozu, M., Moulding, R., Shams, G., Sica, C., Simos, G. and Wong, W. (2014), 'You can run but you can't hide: intrusive thoughts on six continents'. *Journal of Obsessive-Compulsive and Related Disorders,* 3(3): 269–279.

amygdala hijack … Goleman, D. (2005), *Emotional Intelligence: Why it can matter more than IQ,* New York: Bantam Books.

When the amygdala … Schafe, G.E., Doyere, V. and LeDoux, J.E. (2005), 'Tracking the fear engram: the lateral amygdala is an essential locus of fear memory storage'. *Journal of Neuroscience,* 25(43): 10010–10014.

mindfulness has the power … Taren, A.A., Creswell, J.D. and Gianaros, P.J. (2013), 'Dispositional mindfulness co-varies with smaller amygdala and caudate volumes in community adults'. *PLOS ONE,* 8(5): e64574.

Chapter 4

I'm very process … Piampiano, S. Author interview 6 March 2017.

Not only did I … Piampiano, S. <https://sarahpiampiano.com/> [Accessed December 2016]

Rory Bosio … Lobby, M. (2013), 'Rory Bosio ultra successful, ambitious'. <http://www.espn.com/espnw/athletes-life/article/10082046/espnw-rory-bosio-raising-ceiling-women-ultra-running-hoping-attract-more-women-sport-way> [Accessed March 2017]

He's even been named … Neuman, C. (2007), 'The TIME 100: Dean Karnazes'. <http://content.time.com/time/specials/2007/time100walkup/article/0,28804,1611030_1610841_1609861,00.html> [Accessed March 2017]

there's magic in … Karnazes, D. (2006), *Ultramarathon Man: Confessions of an all-night runner,* New York: Penguin Random House

About ten years ago … Karnazes, D. Author interview 8 February, 2017.

Mindfulness can help … Hecht, R. Author interview 15 March, 2017.

the intensity of pain is … Kabat-Zinn, J. (1990), *Full Catastrophe Living,* New York: Bantam Books.

thoughts associated with pain … Samson, A., Simpson, D., Kamphoff, C. and Langlier, A. (2014), 'Think aloud: An examination of runners' thought processes'. *International Journal of Sport and Exercise Psychology,* 15(2): 176–189.

memories of suffering … Babel, P. (2016), 'Memory of pain induced by physical exercise'. *Memory,* 24(4): 548–559.

research involving ultra runners … Simpson, D., Post, P.G., Young, G. and Jensen, P.R. (2014), 'It's not about taking the easy road: The experiences of ultramarathon runners'. *Sport Psychologist,* 28(2): 176–185.

shown to reduce pain … Zeidan, F., Grant, J.A., Brown, C.A., McHaffie, J.G. and Coghill, R.C. (2012), 'Mindfulness meditation-related pain relief: Evidence for unique brain mechanisms in the regulation of pain'. *Neuroscience Letters,* 520 (2): 165–173.

therapeutic techniques rooted … Martin, E.C., Galloway-Williams, N., Cox, M.G. and Winett, R.A. (2015), 'Pilot testing of a mindfulness- and acceptance-based intervention for increasing cardiorespiratory fitness in sedentary adults: A feasibility study'. *Journal of Contextual Behavioral Science,* 4(4): 237–245.

just four sessions … Zeidan, F., Martucci, K.T., Kraft, R.A., Gordon, N.S., McHaffie, J.G. and Coghill, R.C. (2011), 'Brain mechanisms supporting modulation of pain by mindfulness meditation'. *Journal of Neuroscience,* 31(14): 5540–5548.

That's pretty amazing … Zeidan, F. (2011), 'Demystifying meditation—brain imaging illustrates how meditation reduces pain'. <http://www.wakehealth. edu/News-Releases/2011/Demystifying_Meditation_Brain_Imaging_ Illustrates_How_Meditation_Reduces_Pain.htm> [Accessed February 2017]

We haven't seen any other … Zeidan, F. Author interview 9 March 2017.

researchers at the University … Lieberman, M.D., Eisenberger, N.I., Crockett, M.J., Tom, S.M., Pfeifer, J.H. and Way, B.M. (2007), 'Putting feelings into words'. *Psychological Science,* 18(5): 421–428.

the better you are at describing … Barrett, L.F., Gross, J., Christensen, R.C. and Benvenuto, M. (2001), 'Knowing what you're feeling and knowing what to do about it: Mapping the relation between emotion differentiation and emotion regulation'. *Cognition and Emotion,* 15(6): 713–724.

we confuse comfort … Karnazes, D. (2006), *Ultramarathon Man: Confessions of an all-night runner,* New York: Penguin Random House

Hill, you're a bitch … Samson, A., Simpson, D., Kamphoff, C. and Langlier, A. (2015), 'Think aloud: An examination of runners' thought processes'. *International Journal of Sport and Exercise Psychology,* 15(2): 176–189.

researchers at the Exercise Physiology … Esteve-Lanao, J., Foster, C., Seiler, S. and Lucia, Al. (2007), 'Impact of training intensity distribution of performance in endurance athletes'. *Journal of Strength and Conditioning Research,* 21(3): 943–949.

Take time to rest … Havey, M. (2015) 'The Wisconsin Chronicles: Overtraining, be gone!' <http://www.ironman.com/triathlon/news/articles/2015/08/the-wisconsin-chronicles-rest-and-recovery.aspx#axzz4XH0x3aiP> [Accessed December 2016] *if you want to be competitive* … Lobby, M. (2009) 'Mind over matter', *Running Times.*

psychobiological model … McCormich, A., Meijen, C. and Marcora, S. (2015), 'Psychological determinants of whole-body endurance performance'. *Sports Medicine,* 45(7): 997–1015.

I don't think we have … Magness, S. Author interview 14 March 2017.

reduce fatigue … Black, D.S., O'Reilly, G.A., Olmstead, R., Breen, E.C. and Irwin, M.R. (2015), 'Mindfulness meditation and improvement in sleep quality and daytime impairment among older adults with sleep disturbances: A randomized clinical trial'. *JAMA Internal Medicine,* 175(4): 494–501.

Coupled with the knowledge … O'Connor, P., Dishman, R. and Puetz, T. (2006), 'Regular exercise plays a consistent and significant role in reducing fatigue'. <https://www.sciencedaily.com/releases/2006/11/061101151005.htm> [Accessed December 2015]

It was the third … 'Hamilton collapses in 1,500m final lap'. <http://olympics.nbcsports.com/2015/09/09/suzy-favor-hamilton-olympic-race-video-fall-collapse-track-and-field-sydney-2000/> [Accessed January 2017]

In her 2015 memoir … Favor Hamilton, S. (2015), *Fast Girl: A life spent running from madness,* New York: Harper Collins.

people with a more adept … Donald, J.N., Atkins, P.W.B., Parker, P.D., Christie, A.M. and Ryan, R.M. (2016), 'Daily stress and the benefits of mindfulness: Examining the daily and longitudinal relations between present-moment awareness and stress responses'. *Journal of Research in Personality,* 65: 30–37.

wanting things to be … Dalai Lama, Tutu, D. and Abrams, D.C. (2016), *The Book of Joy: Lasting Happiness in a changing world,* New York: Penguin Random House.

champion track cyclist … Ewing, S. (2008), 'Olympic hero Chris Hoy plagued by panic attacks. Then he found an unlikely cure…'. <http://www.dailymail.co.uk/health/article-1100491/Like-thousands-Britons-Olympic-hero-Chris-Hoy-plagued-panic-attacks-Then-unlikely-cure-.html> [Accessed December 2016]

To address these feelings … Peters, S. (2013), *The Chimp Paradox: The mind management program to help you achieve success, confidence, and happiness,* New York: Penguin.

how heavy-handed anxiety … Kleine, D., Sampedro, R.M. and Melo, S.L. (1988), 'Anxiety and performance in runners: Effects of stress and anxiety on physical performance'. *Anxiety Research,* 1(3): 235–246.

how heavy-handed anxiety … Krane, V. (1993), 'A practical application of the anxiety-athletic performance relationship: The zone of optimal functioning hypothesis'. *The Sport Psychologist,* 7(2): 113–126.

If you're not being … Smith, L. Author interview 13 March 2017.

eustress and distress … Lazarus, R.S. (1966), *Psychological Stress and the Coping Process,* New York: McGraw Hill.

Posited by psychologists … Yerkes, R.M. and Dodson, J.D. (1908), 'The relation of strength of stimulus to rapidity of habit-formation'. *Journal of Comparative Neurology and Psychology,* 18(50): 459–482.

Imagine an inverted … Hanin, Y.L. (2000), *Emotions in Sport,* Champaign, IL: Human Kinetics.

Sian Beilock's work ... Beilock, S. (2011), *Choke: What the secrets of the brain reveal about getting it right when you have to,* New York: Free Press.

Reframing anxiety ... Brooks, A.W. (2014), 'Get excited: Reappraising pre-performance anxiety as excitement'. *Journal of Experimental Psychology,* 143(3): 1144–1158.

psychotherapy studies ... Shedler, J. (2010), 'The efficacy of psychodynamic psychotherapy'. *American Psychologist,* 65(2): 98–109.

Whatever approach you ... Oudejans, R.R., Kuijpers, W., Kooijman, C.C. and Bakker, F. (2011), 'Thoughts and attention of athletes under pressure: skill-focus or performance worries?' *Anxiety, Stress, & Coping,* 24(1): 59–73.

Gale force winds ... Bannister, R. (2014), *Twin Tracks: The Autobiography,* London: Robson Press.

like an exploded ... Bannister, R. (1980), *The First Four Minutes,* London: Sutton Publishing.

impediment to achieving flow ... Delrue, J., Mouratidis, A., Haerens, L., De Muyunck, G.-J., Aelterman, N. and Vansteenkiste, M. (2016), 'Intrapersonal achievement goals and underlying reasons among long distance runners: Their relation with race experience, self-talk, and running time'. *Psychologica Belgica,* 56(3): 288–310.

motivational self talk ... Blanchfield, A.W., Hardy, J., DeMorree, H.M., Staiano, W. and Marcora, S.M. (2014), 'Talking yourself out of exhaustion: the effects of self-talk on endurance performance'. *Medicine & Science in Sports & Exercise,* 46(5): 998–1007.

When Spanish researchers ... Briñol, P., Gascó, M., Petty, R.E. and Horcajo, J. (2013), 'Treating thoughts as material objects can increase or decrease their impact on evaluation'. *Psychological Science,* 24(1): 41–47.

self-compassion can be ... Seppälä, E. (2016), *The Happiness Track: How to apply the science of happiness to accelerate your success,* New York: HarperCollins.

Socratic questioning ... Dust, S.B. (2015), 'Mindfulness, flow, and mind wandering: The role of trait-based mindfulness in state-task alignment'. *Industrial and Organizational Psychology,* 8(4): 609–614.

having a few practiced ... Blanchfield, A.W., Hardy, J., DeMorree, H.M., Staiano, W. and Marcora, S.M. (2014), 'Talking yourself out of exhaustion: the effects of self-talk on endurance performance'. *Medicine & Science in Sports & Exercise,* 46(5): 998–1007.

athlete's sense of ... Schunk, D.H. (1995), 'Self-efficacy, motivation, and performance'. *Journal of Applied Sport Psychology,* 7(2): 112–137.

athlete's sense of ... Moritz, S.E., Feltz, D.L., Fahrbach, K.R. and Mack, D.E. (2000), 'The relation of self-efficacy measures to sport performance: a meta-analytic review'. *Research Quarterly for Exercise and Sport,* 71(3): 280–294.

put athletes through ... Kaufman, K.A., Glass, C.R. and Arnkoff, D.B. (2009), 'Evaluation of mindful sport performance enhancement (MPSE): A new approach to promote flow in athletes'. *Journal of Clinical Sports Psychology,* 4: 334–356.

Janet Cherobon-Bawcom ... Lobby, M. (2013) 'Twists, turns, titles for elite runner'. <http://www.espn.com/espnw/athletes-life/article/9911358/espnw-janet-

cherobon-bawcom-arrives-new-york-city-marathon-starting-line-kenya>
[Accessed November 2016]

Danish philosopher … Kierkegaard, S. (1992), *Either/Or: A fragmented life,* New York: Penguin Books.

researchers from the University … Wilson, T.D., Reinhard, D.A., Westgate, E.C., Gilbert, D.T., Ellerbeck, N., Hahn, C., Brown, C.L. and Shaked, A. (2014), 'Just think: The challenges of the disengaged mind'. *Science,* 345(6192): 75–77.

mixing up the types … Sylvester, B.D., Standage, M., McEwan, D., Wolf, S.A., Lubans, D.R., Eather, N. Kaulius, M., Ruissen, G.R., Crocker, P.R.E., Zumbo, B.D. and Beauchamp, M.R. (2016), 'Variety support and exercise adherence behavior: experimental and mediating effects'. *Journal of Behavioral Medicine,* 39(2): 214–224.

mixing up the types … Coon, J.T., Boddy, K., Stein, K., Whear, R., Barton, J. and Depledge, M.H. (2011), 'Does participating in physical activity in outdoor natural environments have a greater effect on physical and mental well-being than physical activity indoors? A systematic review'. *Environmental Science & Technology,* 45(5): 1761–1772.

people tended to enjoy … Heisz, J.J., Tejada, M.G.M., Paolucci, E.M. and Muir, C. (2016), 'Enjoyment for high-intensity interval exercise increases during the first six weeks of training: implications for promoting exercise adherence in sedentary adults'. *PLOS One,* 11(12): e0168534.

South Indian Monkey Trap … Pirsig, R.M. (2006), *Zen and the Art of Motorcycle Maintenance: An inquiry Into values,* New York: HarperTorch.

nonattachment contributes … Sahdra, B.K., Shaver, P.R. and Brown, K.W. (2010), 'A scale to measure nonattachment: a Buddhist complement to Western research on attachment and adaptive functioning'. *Journal of Personality Assessment,* 92(2): 116–127.

identified an inverse … Ju, S.J. and Lee, W.K. (2015), 'Mindfulness, non-attachment, and emotional well-being in Korean adults'. *Advanced Science and Technology Letters,* 87: 68–72.

attention tends to … Smallwood, J., Beach, E., Schooler, J.W. and Handy, T.C. (2008), 'Going AWOL in the brain: mind wandering reduces cortical analysis of external events'. *Journal of Cognitive Neuroscience,* 20(3): 458–469.

some amount of daydreaming … Levinson, D.B., Smallwood, J. and Davidson, R.J. (2012), 'The persistence of thought'. *Psychological Science,* 23(4): 375–380.

demonstrated that mind wandering … Baird, B., Smallwood, J., Mrazek, M.D., Kam, J.W., Franklin, M.S. and Schooler, J.W. (2012), 'Inspired by distraction: mind wandering facilitates creative incubation'. *Psychological Science,* 23(10): 1117–1122.

Chapter 5

I knew this … O'Brien, J. (2011) <http://www.johnhancock.com/bostonmarathon/mediaguide/10-marathoninreview.php> [Accessed January 2017]

It's that place … Young, J.A. and Pain, M.D. (1999), 'The Zone: Evidence of a universal phenomenon for athletes across sports'. *Athletic Insight.*

When I ran … Hall, R. Author interview 22 August 2016.

Back in the 1970s … Csikszentmihalyi, M. (1992), *Optimal Experience: Psychological studies of flow in consciousness,* Cambridge: Cambridge University Press.

The flow state … Keflezighi, M. Author interview 14 May 2017.

It is a quasi … Pollock, P. Author interview 22 March 2017.

I've found that … Conley, K. Author interview 16 February 2017.

When I am in … Ahmed, M. Author interview 1 March 2017.

An energy overcomes … Jones, R. Author interview 23 March 2017.

When I'm running … Pappas, A. Author interview 23 March 2017.

The flow experience … Adams, L. Author interview 16 February 2017.

I think in the flow … Petty, A. Author interview 14 March 2017.

When I'm in … Davis, C. Author interview 26 March 2017.

Being in the zone … Yelling, L. Author interview 23 March 2017.

the flow experience is autotelic … Csikszentmihalyi, M., Latter, P. & Duranso, C.W. (2017), *Running Flow: Mental immersion techniques for better running,* Illinois: Human Kinetics.

when we are in … Csikszentmihalyi, M. (1990), *Flow: The psychology of optimal experience,* New York: Harper and Row.

hedonic happiness … Ryan, R.M. and Deci, E.L. (2001), 'On happiness and human potentials: a review of research on hedonic and eudaimonic well-being'. *Annual Review of Psychology,* 52:141–166.

Research by psychologists … Huta, V. and Ryan, R.M. (2010), 'Pursuing pleasure or virtue: The differential and overlapping well-being benefits of hedonic and eudaimonic motives'. *Journal of Happiness Studies,* 11(6): 735–762.

Mindfulness is a state … Benzo, R. Author Interview 21 March 2017.

A heightened state … Young, J.A. & Pain, M.D. (1999), 'The zone: evidence of a universal phenomenon for athletes across sports'. *Athletic Insight,* (1)3: 21–30.

Achieving flow … Keflezighi, M. Author interview 14 May 2017.

as little as a month … Kaufman, K.A., Glass, C.R. and Arnkoff, D.B. (2009), 'Evaluation of mindful sport performance enhancement (MPSE): A new approach to promote flow in athletes'. *Journal of Clinical Sports Psychology,* 4: 334–356.

It starts with … Kastor, D. Author interview 4 April 2017.

flow is attained … Csikszentmihalyi, M., Latter, P. and Duranso, C.W. (2017), *Running Flow: Mental immersion techniques for better running,* Illinois: Human Kinetics.

right on the top … Csikszentmihalyi, M. (1998). *Finding Flow: The psychology of engagement with everyday life,* New York: Basic Books.

a few studies have … Schucker, L. Hagemann, N. & Strauss, B. (2013), 'Attentional processes and choking under pressure'. *Perceptual and Motor Skills,* 116(2): 671–689.

Flow, in life … Benzo, R. (2016) <https://connect.mayoclinic.org/discussion/5-mindfulness-and-flow/> [Accessed January 2017]

a million mulligans … Harris, D. (2014), *10% Happier: How I tamed the voice in my head, reduced stress without losing my edge, and found self-help that actually works—A true story,* New York: Harper Collins.

Chapter 6

Racing has taught me … Yelling, L. Author interview 23 March 2017.

it's just running … Wightman, S. (2016) <http://www.flyingrunner.co.uk/liz-yelling-shares-lessons-learnt-about-training-competing-and-coaching/> [Accessed March 2017]

Running taught me … Yelling, L. Author interview 23 March 2017.

As Pappas says … Pappas, A. (2016) 'Speed Goggles'. <http://www.flotrack.org/article/44578-watch-all-of-alexi-pappas-s-speed-goggles-shorts#.WOMlVY61to4> [Accessed January 2017]

We often get nervous … Kamphoff, C. Author interview 3 April 2017.

a predictable pre-race … Hazell, J., Cotterill, S.T. and Hill, D.M. (2014), 'An exploration of pre-performance routines, self-efficacy, anxiety and performance in semi-professional soccer'. *European Journal of Sport Science*, 14(6): 603–610.

focus and attention … Lazar, S.W., Bush, G., Gollub, R.L., Fricchione, G.L., Khalsa, G. and Benson, H. (2000), 'Functional brain mapping of the relaxation response and meditation'. *Neuroreport*, 11(7): 1581–1585.

counteract stress … Kuo, B., Bhasin, M., Jacquart, J., Scult, M.A., Slipp, L., Riklin, E.I., Lepoutre, V., Comosa, N., Norton, B-A., Dassatti, A., Rosenblum, J., Thurler, A.H., Surjanhata, B.C., […] and Denninger, J.W. (2015), 'Genomic and clinical effects associated with a relaxation response mind-body intervention in patients with irritable bowel syndrome and inflammatory bowel disease'. *PLOS One*, 10(4):e0123861.

reduce blood pressure … Joseph, C.N., Porta, C., Casucci, G., Casiraghi, N., Maffeis, M., Rossi, M. and Bernardi, L. (2005), 'Slow breathing improves arterial baroreflex sensitivity and decreases blood pressure in essential hypertension'. *Hypertension*, 46(4): 714–718.

regulate heart rate … Keefer, L. and Blanchard, E.B. (2001), 'The effects of relaxation response meditation on the symptoms of irritable bowel syndrome: results of a controlled treatment study'. *Behaviour Research and Therapy*, 39(7): 801–811.

it also has the power … Hafenbrack, A.C., Kinias, Z and Barsade, S.G. (2014), 'Debiasing the mind through meditation: mindfulness and the sunk-cost bias'. *Psychological Science*, 25(2): 369–376.

if you're feeling nervous … Brown, R.P. and Gerbarg, P.L. (2012), *The Healing Power of Breath: Simple techniques to reduce stress and anxiety, enhance concentration, and balance your emotions*, Boston: Shambhala.

likens the breath … Kabat-Zinn, J. (1990), *Full Catastrophe Living*, New York: Bantam Books.

Since we know that … Gergley, J.C. (2013), 'Acute effect of passive static stretching on lower-body strength in moderately trained men'. *Journal of Strength and Conditioning Research*, 27(4): 973–977.

They emphasize good form … Turner, A.M., Owings, M. and Schwane, J.A. (2003), 'Improvement in running economy after 6 weeks of plyometric training'. *Journal of Strength and Conditioning Research*, 17(1): 60–67.

these types of drills ... Davies, G., Reimann, B.L. and Manske, R. (2015), 'Current concepts of plyometric exercise'. *International Journal of Sports Physical Therapy*, 10(6): 760–786.

these types of drills ... Chimera, N.J., Swanik, K.A., Swanik, C.B. and Straub, S.J. (2004), 'Effects of plyometric training on muscle-activation strategies and performance in female athletes'. *Journal of Athletic Training*, 39(1): 24–31.

She began to stagger ... Strout, E. (2016) 'Shalane Flanagan on dehydration, delirium, and drama at the Olympic Trials'. *Runner's World Magazine*. <http://www.runnersworld.com/olympic-trials/shalane-flanagan-on-dehydration-delirium-and-drama-at-the-olympic-trials> [Accessed January 2017]

I might be ... Kampf, H. Author interview 15 August 2016.

The YouTube video ... Dorniden, H. (2008) <https://www.youtube.com/watch?v=xjejTQdK5OI> [Accessed March 2017]

brain-body ... Burfoot, A. (2013). 'How to run your best marathon pace'. *Runner's World*. <http://www.runnersworld.com/peak-performance/how-to-run-your-best-marathon-pace-guaranteed> [Accessed January 2017]

freak-out moments ... Magness, S. Author interview 15 March 2017.

Paula Radcliffe uses ... Murphy, S.M. (2012) *The Oxford Handbook of Sport and Performance Psychology*. Oxford: Oxford University Press.

keeping a gratitude journal ... Emmons, R.A. and Mishra, A. (2011), 'Why gratitude enhances well-being', in *Designing Positive Psychology: Taking stock and moving forward*. Oxford: Oxford University Press.

Saudi Arabian Olympian ... Attar, S. Author interview 28 February 2017.

Refrain from reflecting ... Petruzzelli, G. Author interview 26 March 2017.

It's really important ... Smith, L. Author interview 9 March 2017.

Chapter 7

When I run ... Davis, C. Author interview 19 March 2017.

It was devastating ... Davis, C. Author interview 19 March 2017.

the hallmark of ... Petruzzelli, G. Author interview 26 March 2017.

Running in Ethiopia ... Wade, R. Author interview 9 March 2017.

I tell the athletes ... Yelling, L. Author interview 23 March 2017.

It's important for ... Fish, E. Author interview 9 March 2017.

A lot of my students ... Magness, S. Author interview 26 March 2017.

If you get wrapped ... Brewer, J. Author interview 16 March 2017.

When there are roots ... Valerio, M. Author interview 14 March, 2017.

Being in the back ... Attar, S. Author interview 28 February 2017.

When you tap into ... Brewer, J. Author interview 16 March 2017.

Mindfulness can help you ... Hecht, R. Author interview March 15, 2017.

This ability to sit ... Taren, A. Author interview March 15, 2017.

Paying attention to ... Kamphoff, C. Author interview 3 April 2017.

I am so inspired ... Attar, S. Author interview 28 February 2017.

When we watch ... Pearson, T. Author interview 5 April 2017.

Even in moments ... Kastor, D. Author interview 4 April 2017.

experiencing things … Zeidan, F. Author interview March 9, 2017.
You have to create … Benzo, R. Author interview 17 March 2017.

Chapter 8

scores of research … Woodyard, C. (2011), 'Exploring the therapeutic effects of yoga and its ability to increase quality of life'. *International Journal of Yoga*, 4(2): 49–54.

scores of research … Smith, C., Hancock, H., Blake-Mortimer, J. and Eckert, K. (2007), 'A randomized comparative trial of yoga and relaxation to reduce stress and anxiety'. *Complementary Therapies in Medicine*, 15(2): 77–83.

scores of research … Brown, R.P. and Gerbarg, P.L. (2005), 'Sudarshan Kriya yogic breathing in the treatment of stress, anxiety, and depression: Part I—neurophysiologic model'. *Journal of Alternative and Complementary Medicine*, 11(1): 189–201.

short moments … Salzberg, S. (2012) <https://www.sharonsalzberg.com/realhappinessblogshort-moments-many-times/> [Accessed March 2017]

INDEX

Praise for Mindful Running

"Mackenzie Havey does a masterful job explaining how mindful running can lead to numerous benefits and result in a more fulfilling workout experience. Her points are well supported with credible research findings and case studies, yet *Mindful Running* is written in understandable language that can be easily adopted by both competitive and everyday runners. A must-read for anyone looking to improve performance and add richer meaning to the sport, activity and art of running."

Dean Karnazes, ultra marathoner and
***NY Times* bestselling author**

"In this age of distraction, we would all benefit from being more present more often. Mackenzie L. Havey shows how and why to achieve this goal in your running, and how that practice can benefit you in your non-running hours."

Scott Douglas, *Runner's World* contributing editor and
bestselling running book author

"*Mindful Running* is the bridge to using your body, mind and surroundings to get the most out of your running…Whether you want running to be more comfortable, you want to run faster or longer, or you want to de-stress while in your running shoes, this book will be your biggest asset."

Deena Kastor, three-time Olympian, 2004 Marathon Bronze
medallist and US record holder in the marathon and half-marathon

"*Mindful Running* will surely inspire many to take up running AND to do so mindfully."

Dr. Tracey J. Shors, Neuroscientist and
Distinguished Professor, Rutgers University

The fastest, happiest, and most durable athletes are those that are able to remain present and think positively, as Mackenzie L. Havey colorfully demonstrates throughout *Mindful Running*. Whether you're seeking to break records, forge friendships, or simply get the best out of yourself through the sport, *Mindful Running* offers a great springboard for your performance and overall well-being."

Becky Wade, professional marathon runner and
author of *Run the World: My 3,500-Mile Journey*
Through Running Cultures Around the Globe

"Mackenzie L. Havey serves up equal parts inspiration and instruction in *Mindful Running*. Runners of all abilities will love the stories she's collected from the sport's greatest heroes, and the scientifically-grounded advice for achieving the genuine, lasting happiness they've found through practicing mindfulness—both in and out of their running shoes."

Erin Beresini, Editor in Chief of *Triathlete Magazine*

"Mackenzie Havey skillfully weaves together the latest scientific research behind mindfulness with real-life tales of runners from all walks of life, resulting in a fascinating and accessible book. If you're curious about applying mindfulness to enhance your performance—and enjoyment—of running, *Mindful Running* will be your guide along the way. The included actionable items allow runners to not only understand why and how mindfulness can help them, but provide practical 'how-to's' that readers will likely want to revisit throughout their athletic careers."

Adrienne Taren, PhD, neuroscientist and mindfulness researcher

"*Mindful Running* is a practical, relatable and down-to-earth guide on how to make mindfulness a part of your daily life and running routine. Mackenzie L. Havey does an excellent job building the foundation for understanding what mindfulness is and why it can benefit your running lifestyle, while at the same time providing inspirational anecdotal stories to keep you engaged. As a seasoned runner and mindfulness practitioner, it was refreshing to read an organized and concise approach on how to get creative with my mindful running practice… *Mindful Running* is a must to add to your training library!"

Dr. Gloria Petruzzelli, Sport Psychologist & USA Track & Field-certified coach

"From the very first page I was hooked. I loved this book: *Mindful Running* gives runners instructions on how to mindfully run with joy and ease. It is inspiring, motivating, fun, warm, and it has a spirit of optimism."

Terry Pearson, RPh, MBA, leading Mindfulness-Based Stress Reduction instructor and clinical researcher